STANLEY J. FARMER:
WE CALLED HIM COACH

Jerry H. Summers

Waldenhouse Publishers, Inc.
Walden, Tennessee

STANLEY J. FARMER: WE CALLED HIM COACH

Copyright ©2017 Jerry H. Summers. All rights reserved. No part of this book may be reproduced in any form or by any electronic or mechanical means including information storage and retrieval systems, without permission in writing from the publisher. The only exception is by a reviewer, who may quote short excerpts in a review.
Published by Waldenhouse Publishers, Inc.
100 Clegg Street, Signal Mountain, Tennessee 37377 USA
Printed in the United States of America
Type and Design by Karen Paul Stone
ISBN: 978-1-935186-92-2
Library of Congress Control Number: 2017911549
  Covers the life of Stanley J. Farmer from his birth on February 13, 1913, to his death on September 18, 1996. Tells of his athletic and coaching career, military service in WWII and his 31 year tenure at Central High School in Chattanooga, Tennessee, as coach, teacher, and principal. 175 illustrations. -- Provided by publisher
BIO019000 BIOGRAPHY & AUTOBIOGRAPHY / Educators
BIO016000 BIOGRAPHY & AUTOBIOGRAPHY / Sports
SPO061020 SPORTS & RECREATION / Coaching / Football
HIS036120 HISTORY / United States / State & Local / South
Other books by this author:
The Turtle and the Lawyer
ISBN: 978-1-935186-62-5 Waldenhouse Publishers, Inc., Walden, TN
Rush to Justice? Tennessee's Forgotten Trial of the Century – Schoolfield 1958.
ISBN: 978-1-935186-63-2 Waldenhouse Publishers, Inc., Walden, TN
Schoolfield: Out of the Ashes
ISBN: 987-1-935186-91-5 Waldenhouse Publishers, Inc., Walden, TN

Dedication

To the memory of Stanley J. and Katherine Farmer
and the thousands of
Central High alumni and supporters
who believe in the eternal "Spirit of Central"

All proceeds from the publication will be donated to the Community Foundation of Greater Chattanooga (CFGC), 1270 Market Street, Chattanooga, TN 37402 to supplement the corpus of the **Stanley J. Farmer scholarship awarded to qualified seniors at Central** to assist them in obtaining college educations. CFGC is a 501(c)(3) duly qualified charity and all funds given to it are tax deductible.

Donations should be designated as follows:
Community Foundation of Greater Chattanooga (CFGC) - Central Stanley J. Farmer Scholarship.

Books can be purchased directly from Summers, Rufolo & Rodgers, 735 Broad Street, Suite 800, Chattanooga, Tennessee 37402 with a check made payable to the CFGC for $21.95 plus $4.00 for shipping, or books can be picked up at the law firm. Please include phone number or e-mail address for order confirmation along with complete name and shipping address.

Table of Contents

Dedication		3
Preface		5
Foreword		6
Acknowledgements		7
The Author		9
I.	The Beginning	11
II.	City High School	17
III.	Emory & Henry College	23
IV.	Back to City High	27
V.	Military Service	33
VI.	Central Coaching Career—1947-1969	49
VII.	Assistant Principal—1970-1977	135
VIII.	Principal—1977-1978	145
IX.	Retirement	157
X.	Post Central Life	167
XI.	Recollection of Players and Students	173
XII.	Sportswriters Reviews	191
XIII.	End of an Era	199
XIV.	Conclusion	207

Preface

The measurement of an individual's success in life has often been described as the effect one has on the lives of others with whom they have come in contact rather than material wealth. If that standard is applied to Coach Stanley J. Farmer, based on the impact he had on the thousands of young men and women with whom he had contact with during his personal, military, educational and athletic careers, he would have to be considered a very wealthy individual.

The accounts of events in his life herein are just a small part of the effect he had on the lives of those students and soldiers who were fortunate enough to have come under his influence. Many of the stories told about how he and his wife, Katherine, helped young men financially, spiritually, and otherwise, have been lost to history due to the passage of time and the death of many of the soldiers, students, and athletes who were fortunate enough to have been connected with Coach Farmer.

The purpose of this book is to share those instances that occurred as we travel down the road of his life. We who knew him would be unanimous in our assessment of him as a great man.

Foreword

The title to this publication, *Stanley J. Farmer – We Called Him Coach* was chosen to show his love and commitment to Chattanooga Central High School from 1947-1996.

Whether it was the old Central that existed on Dodds Avenue from 1907-1968 or the present school on Highway 58 that is still in existence in 2017 after its inaugural class in 1969, Stan Farmer was at both schools equally committed to the preservation of the "Central Spirit" that is a signature symbol of the school. Stan Farmer loved both schools and gave his all to each institution of learning until his death in 1996.

He was the "Real Central Connection" and it is hoped that his commitment in this publication will eliminate the distinction between "old" Central and "new" Central.

Stan Farmer unequivocally believed in the following part of the *alma mater*-"What A Wonderful School – Central High."

Jerry H. Summers, 2017

Acknowledgements

No publication can be written without the help and support of many people. This venture into a literary endeavor about the life of Stanley J. Farmer was no exception.

Melinda Martin, librarian at Central High School performed yeomans work to satisfy my numerous requests for documents in the Central memorabilia and archives pertaining to Coach Farmer. The library staff at Central was of great assistance in making available the copies of the Central annual, *The Champion*, from 1947-1978 which covered the term of service at the school by Coach Farmer.

The *Chattanooga Times* and *Chattanooga News-Free Press* have preserved on microfilm at the Hamilton County Bicentennial Library additional historical data under the leadership of head librarian, Corrine Hill, and her staff of Mary Nelms, April Mitchell, Jim Reece, Jennifer Rydell, and Suzette Raney were all of great help in our research efforts.

Retired sportswriters Sam Woolwine, Buck Johnson, Roy Exum, Ward Gossett, Dan Cook, Stephen Hargis and Randy Smith contributed significant information acquired in their sports coverage of Central and Coach Farmer over the years. The late *Chattanooga Times* columnist Bill Casteel also interviewed "Coach."

Coach Farmer's widow and soulmate, Katherine Phillips Farmer, provided me with much personal and historical information in the many telephone conversations we had until her untimely death on September 25, 2016.

Kathy Farmer Ratz, daughter of Stan and Katherine, helped me in conversations with her mother and others for memorable instances that needed to be preserved for posterity and the history of her father and Central High School. Diane Hale, former guidance counselor and close personal friends of the Farmers graciously conveyed her knowledge of that friendship over the years.

The many former athletes and students at Central who responded to my request for stories of their contact with Coach Farmer and his wife were very helpful. Some were humorous, some serious, but all were invaluable in helping me to paint the real picture of Stan Farmer's life. Unfortunately others did not contribute their personal stories of their experiences with the Farmers. Many would have further enriched the history of this unique couple.

Karen Stone at Waldenhouse Publishers contributed her expertise and professional advice and criticism.

My longtime friend, Tom Griscom, newspaper man extraordinaire and former confidant of President Ronald Reagan and Senator Howard Baker, Jr., once again suffered through the ordeal of reviewing and editing my work.

Nick Walker, my paralegal, patiently revised my many additions and revisions while continuing to perform his legal work for the firm.

Lastly, I would be remiss if I didn't share my personal relationship with Stan and Katherine Farmer which began in June, 1956 and continued throughout their lifetimes. As he was approaching the end of his life he asked me to keep an eye on Katherine and Kathy. As a result I developed the weekly habit of calling Katherine each Saturday to check on her. Some of those conversations were humorous, some were heated, but all contributed to my final conclusion that this outspoken companion to Coach Farmer was an important part of their undying love for the students and athletes at Central High School. She may have been misunderstood by some, but she was part of the complete devotion of her and Coach Farmer to the needs of many poor and unfortunate young boys and girls whose lives were touched and impacted by them.

The Author

Jerry H. Summers is a practicing attorney in Chattanooga, Tennessee. He has served as an assistant district attorney and municipal judge since he began the practice of law in 1966. His entire life has been lived in Chattanooga, Tennessee except for seven years in St. Petersburg, Florida between the ages of seven and fourteen.

He has argued cases before the United States and Tennessee Supreme courts and has been involved in numerous landmark decisions in both civil and criminal law.

His peers in the legal profession have elected him to membership in the International Academy of Trial Lawyers, American College of Trial Lawyers, International Society of Barristers, American Board of Trial Advocates, American

Board of Criminal Lawyers, and he has been selected every year since 1983 as one of the Best Lawyers in America, in both personal injury and criminal law.

By an unsolicited vote of the lawyers of Tennessee, he has consistently been selected as one of the "Best 100 Lawyers in Tennessee" and "Mid-South Super Lawyers".

Orange Grove Center and the Chattanooga Bar Association have both honored him as philanthropist of the year for his community work.

In 2007 he was selected as a Distinguished Alumnus at the Centennial Celebration of Central High School. In 2014 he was honored by being designated as the Distinguished Alumnus at the University of the South at Sewanee, and in 2016 the University of Tennessee at Knoxville designated him as one of the Distinguished Alumnus at that institution.

This is his third published book. His first, *The Turtle and the Lawyer* released in 2014, is an attempt to thank those individuals and entities that have helped him in life and to respectfully suggest that the reader do the same. His second, published in 2016, is a biography of the controversial life of Judge Raulston Schoolfield titled *Rush to Justice? Tennessee's Forgotten Trial of the Century – Schoolfield 1958*. In publication is a sequel: *Schoolfield: Out of the Ashes*.

Chapter I

The Beginning

On February 13, 1913, Mr. and Mrs. Frank W. Farmer were blessed with the birth of a three pound male child who would grow into the legend described in this publication. The elderly black lady that cleaned him up when he was born gave the baby a dose of Castor oil and stated to his parents that he would grow up to be their largest child. The family resided in the St. Elmo section of Chattanooga, Tennessee.

Brothers Stewart, Stan and Frank Farmer. Courtesy of Farmer Family.

Stan with his parents, Mr. and Mrs. Frank Farmer. Photo courtesy of Farmer Family.

Stan had two older brothers, Frank and Stewart, and a sister Betty. The brothers played football at Central and Betty graduated from Central's main rival, City High School in Class of 1934. Stan became an Eagle Scout and in that capacity, he and his brother, Stewart, along with several other scouts were asked to serve as part of a security unit when famed aviator Charles Lindbergh landed at Marr Field in East Chattanooga

Sister Betty with Stan Farmer. Photo courtesy of Farmer Family.

St. Elmo Eagle Scout Troup guarding "Spirit of St. Louis" at Marr Field, October 5, 1927. Courtesy of George Campbell.

on October 5, 1927, after his famous flight from New York to Paris, France, in the "Spirit of St. Louis" monoplane.

After the New York-Paris record breaking flight a tour throughout the country and the Caribbean was scheduled to promote the development of aviation in America and that is how Chattanooga became one of the stops on the itinerary.

Actually, Chattanooga was a substitute stop for Lindbergh's trip as he was initially going to Nashville. However, the sudden death of Governor Henry Horton caused the aviator to make his Tennessee stop in Chattanooga rather than divert attention from the Governor's funeral.

While Lindbergh participated in an open car motorcade to downtown Chattanooga to be honored by Mayor Ed Bass and other dignitaries, the eighteen member Boy Scout troop from St. Elmo Methodist Church guarded the plane while it was being serviced by Lindbergh's escort plane pilot, Phil Love.

Other scouts who guarded the plane included Arthur Hitchcock, John Vass, Elmer Farmer, Burch Cooke, Warren Smith, Roy Smith, Fritz Englehardt, and Wallace Page.

Stan's older brother, Stewart, known as "Plowboy," had been an outstanding football player at Central and Stan wanted to follow in his brother's footsteps. Unfortunately Stanley had grown into a tall skinny specimen weighing only 115 pounds, and Central Coach Dean Peterson decided that he was too small to play football and declined to give him a uniform.

Therefore he enrolled at City High, and although he wanted to go to Central, his father informed him that he would not be able to transfer once he entered City. What followed was a remarkable football career with the Dynamos under Coach Jim Puckett.

Upon graduation he went to Emory and Henry and graduated in four years in 1937.

After receiving his degree at Emory and Henry he worked for a trucking company for a year before he returned to Chattanooga and coached at City High School for three years and then entered Columbia University in New York where he earned a Master's Degree in Education.

In 1947 he joined the faculty and coaching staff at Central under E.B. Etter, and the rest is sports history.

1939 All-Southern at City. Photo courtesy of City High School.

Chapter II

City High School

When Central football coach Dean Peterson refused to give Stan Farmer a football uniform the decision would come back to haunt the Purple Pounders and benefit the Dynamos. City coach Jim Puckett had no problem with giving the lanky freshman an opportunity to play on the football team.

By his senior year Stan had grown to 156 pounds and was the star of the City team. He started at center for four years at the school on 3rd Street. During his sophomore year he was selected to the second team for the All City team and was the first team center on the All City team during his junior and senior years. During his senior year he was chosen for the All State and All Southern squads. The recognition for the latter was the only City player to ever receive this honor in the history of the school.

A high honor he received that indicated his popularity with his teammates and coaching staff was when he was selected captain during his senior year for the City-Central game. City won the annual battle with the Purple Pounders, 13-0, and it "broke a long purple reign."

The play of Stan Farmer in the game was described by an enthusiastic writer in the 1933 school annual: "When Central was in possession of the ball, that afforded Stanley Farmer an opportunity to do his stuff. And boy, did he function. He was like a bloodhound tracing the odor of a well-done T-bone steak. And he didn't stop until he had his man. It is the opinion of the writer that the boys from Central do not, in the future, want to play with anyone that has even a rural appearance, much less a rural name. The victory was one of those things in life that cannot be avoided."

He was also selected as captain on the area coaches' All City team in recognition of earning four varsity letters for the Maroon Dynamos.

The school annual described Stan Farmer at the end of his senior year as, "The greatest of all Maroon centers who closed his career in a blaze of glory," after that year's victory over Central in the season finale.

Football was not the only activity that Stan engaged in while at City. He performed in both the junior and senior class plays which later led to some speculation that he developed some of his motivation procedures while performing on the stage. He performed in the junior class play, "Tiger House," a mystery comedy in three acts.

The senior class play, "The Queen's Husband," which took place during the administration of American president Calvin Coolidge, also included a part for Stan as General Northup, premier of England. It was a sophisticated comedy with the events taking place in a mythical and anonymous kingdom situated on an island in the North Sea, somewhere between Denmark and Scotland.

Unfortunately his strongest persuasive techniques were not learned from his thespian performances. A well-placed boot to the posterior of his football players and an equally well placed paddle to the posterior of students were the best motivators that he used during his lengthy coaching and teaching career. The afore-described gestures were usually followed by a big bear hug and friendly smile that let the offender know that Stan Farmer cared about them.

He was also chosen by his classmates to write the "Last Will and Testament of the Class of 1933" as Class Attorney.

A poem written about the senior class entitled "Those 33 Seniors" included a paragraph about Stan Farmer. At the annual Senior Luncheon he gave a speech which was jokingly panned by the Maroon and White students newspaper and his talk was satirically described as "like a rolly on toast," delivered as a partly phrased conglomeration of uninitiated nonsense.

> The most popular athlete I know,
> Stanley Farmer just leads them all,
> He can't be beat at playing ball;
> He and Osmo are one and all.
>
> They play the game and play it fair;
> And always try to dot their share.
> To fill the gap that they will leave,
> Will be a hard task, I do believe.

Stan was also elected president of the Student Council in 1932 as well as vice president of the senior class. He served as

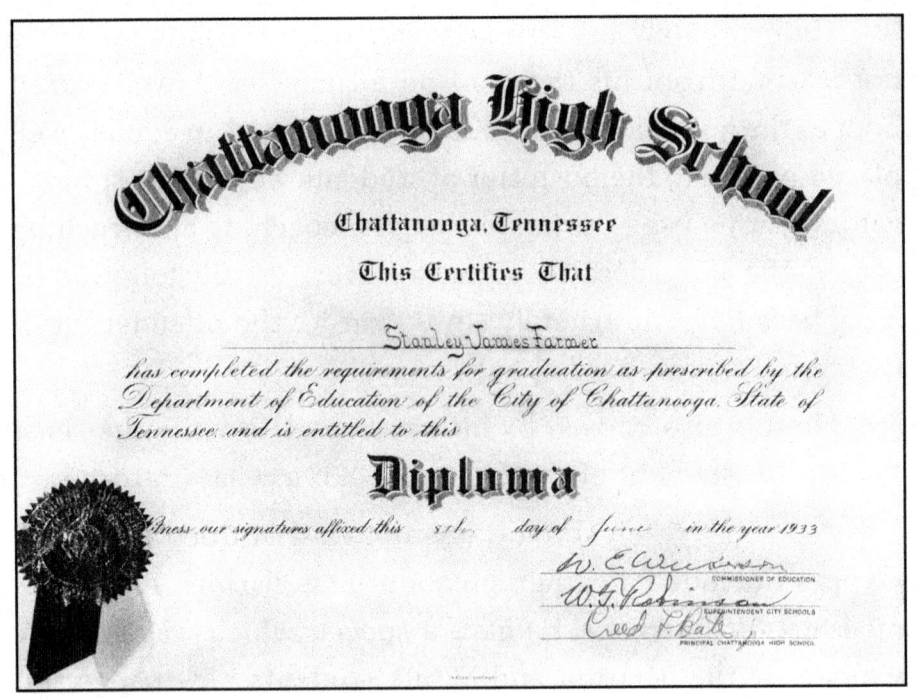

City High School diploma. Courtesy of Farmer family.

president of the Letterman's Club in 1932 and as a Major in the Reserve Officers Training Corps.

The history of the Class of '32 as written by Mary Glen Walker contains a riddle that remains unsolved, as no one can explain the statement, "The history of our class would not be complete, however, without at least the mention of Stanley Farmer, whom the class was sorry to lose at midterm."

That statement, if accurate, remains a mystery to the Farmer family.

Other versions of this gap in Stan's academic background is the allegation that during his junior year at City he entered the United States Marine Corps for two years, then returned to City for his senior year. His diploma from City indicates that he graduated in 1933. The military records from the National Personnel Records Center do not contain any date of enlistment prior to June 21, 1941.

In an interview by *Chattanooga News-Free Press* reporter Dan Cook on September 7, 1980, he states that after Stan graduated from Emory and Henry in 1937, he returned to City High School in Chattanooga and coached and taught history for an additional three years.

The mystique surrounding Coach Stanley J. Farmer evidently began at an early age.

Center Stan Farmer, Emory & Henry 1933. Courtesy of Emory & Henry.

Chapter III

Emory & Henry College

Stanley J. Farmer's father demanded that his son accept the athletic scholarship offered to him at Emory & Henry College in Emory, Virginia, rather than one offered to him at New Orleans University in the fall of 1933. Mr. Farmer took Stan to the train station and put him on the train going to Virginia at the last minute.

The basis for his dad's demand was that Emory and Henry was affiliated with the United Methodist Church and New Orleans University was Catholic. As the superintendent of the St. Elmo Methodist Church, Mr. Farmer had no intention of sending his son to a non-protestant institution of higher learning such as New Orleans University.

Founded in 1836 Emory and Henry is now the highest ranked liberal arts college in the State of Virginia and is the oldest institution of higher learning in Southwest Virginia. It was named after Bishop John Emory of the Methodist Church and American patriot Patrick Henry. It is located in the Virginia Highlands, is surrounded by mountains and numerous rivers, and was accessible by train from Chattanooga in 1933.

The official mascot of the school is the Wasp and it is believed that the name derived out of a football contest between Emory and Henry and the University of Tennessee at Neyland Stadium. Although the Volunteers won the game 27-0, the smaller school held the bigger school scoreless in the first half and the Knoxville paper has been cited for the adoption of the mascot when it reported, "Those Virginia boys stung like Wasps."

Stan Farmer did well at Emory and Henry amid the comments in his yearbooks. His team and classmates indicated that he was well-liked by his fellow students although he was often kidded about being from Tennessee. From the comments of several of the co-eds in the annual it appears he was very popular with the ladies. He acquired the nicknames "Buck" and "Playboy" from the co-eds and his fraternity brothers in *Dom I Necher*, which was unique to Emory and Henry.

The fraternity takes its name from Saint Dominic, the patron saint of astrologers. The first chapter had been formed in 1920 and was "local," meaning that they only existed on the Emory and Henry campuses and did not have any national affiliation. He served as secretary-treasurer and president of the chapter.

The entries in the school annual, "The Sphinx," by his male colleagues wished him well in his coaching career.

He was president of his senior class in 1937, a member of the Blue Key leadership fraternity, president of his fraternity, president of the Men's Pan-Hellenic Counsel, member of the Discipline Committee, and a football lettermen for three years.

The class tribute to him was complimentary: "Great floodlights, a packed stadium and Stanley seem to cling together as a closely connected group in the memories of his many friends. And, too, his leadership will be a distinct asset in later life."

He was also known as a great prankster. He shared stories with his family as to how he and others would shine spotlights on the campus night watchman and trace his steps all night long. Hanging beds out of the windows on the second floor of the dormitories was an admitted college prank.

Stanley James Farmer as a Senior. Photo courtesy of Emory & Henry College.

Another college memory dealt with his fraternity initiation. He was given a box of matches and dropped off at a remote cemetery at midnight on a cold night where he had to kneel down and obtain the names of the dead on the tombstones. Finally, at the last one, he felt something grab him from behind, tugging at his shoulders. He couldn't move as he knelt trying to read the last name by match light and was scared s _ _ _ _ _ _ _. When he tried to get up from his kneeling position, he couldn't. He finally recognized that the heels of his shoes were on the tail of his overcoat restricting all upward movement!

He graduated from Emory and Henry in the summer of 1937 with a B.A. degree.

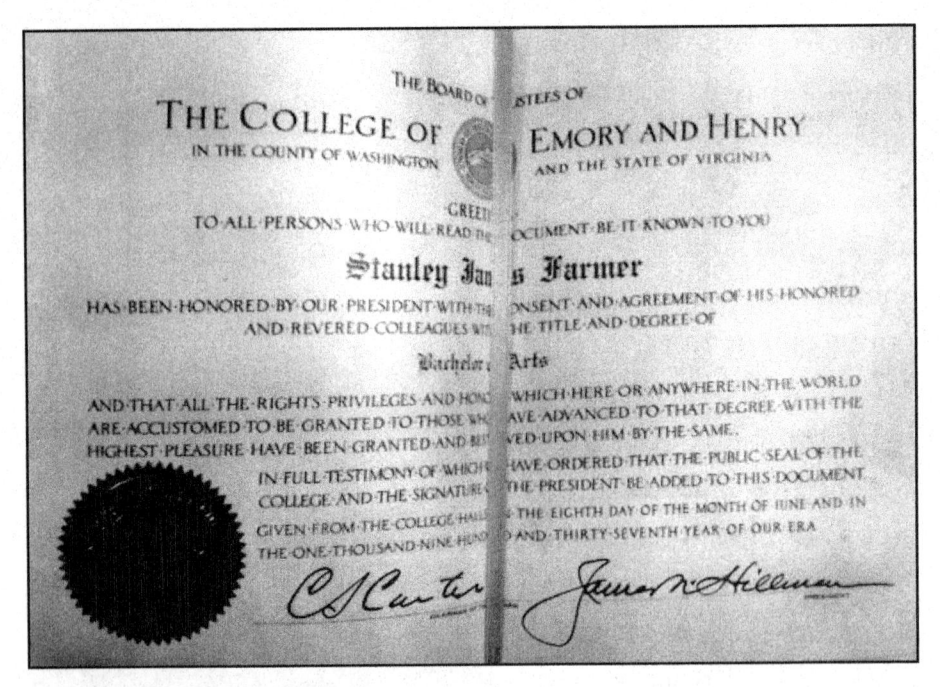

Diploma from Emory & Henry

    Perhaps the recollection of his college past contributed to his willingness not to severely punish minor infractions of school rules when he was assistant principal and principal from 1970-1978. More severe violations were dealt more harshly with his wooden paddle not so affectionately named by the students as the "Board of Education."

Chapter IV

Back to City High

Upon graduating from Emory and Henry, Stan returned to his high school *alma mater*, City High in Chattanooga, in the fall of 1937.

He taught and coached for two years then enlisted in the Navy on June 21, 1941, as a Chief Petty Officer.

He went to Columbia University in the summers of 1938-1939 to obtain a Master's Degree in Physical Education. His explanation to his family as to why he chose that institution of higher education, "Was so that he could attend the World's Fair in New York City in 1939-1940!" He could have gotten the advanced degree at Peabody in Nashville, but the prospect of spending two summers in the "Big Apple" was more appealing.

While there he also went to the rematch of the boxing fight between American heavyweight champion, Joe Louis and German fighter Max Schmeling. Schmeling had knocked Louis out in 1936 when the Brown Bomber was undefeated. The second fight was over quickly, as Louis knocked the German out in two minutes and four seconds.

Coach Farmer later related to his family, "He sure didn't get his money's worth from what was supposed to be a really big fight."

Joe Lewis - Max Schmeling program, 1938. Courtesy of Farmer Family

His brother, Stewart, also attended Columbia during the summers to get his master's degree in physical education. Evidently the two brothers had a lot of non-educational fun and Stewart wound up eating hot dogs for substance. However, he like his younger brother, was highly thought of and respected

Coach of City High basketball team. Photo courtesy of City High.

Basketball coach. Photo courtesy of City High.

Coach of basketball team at City High. Photo courtesy of City High.

Line coach at City High. Photo courtesy of Cith High.

at the high school he taught and coached. A scholarship is given each year in Stewart Farmer's name; the football field is named after him, as well as is a trophy case.

While at City in 1939, Stan guided the junior basketball team to the city title and developed some fine prospects for the next year's varsity team. He also assisted Coach Puckett with the football team and coached the track squad.

The late Lee. S. Anderson, editor of the *Chattanooga News-Free Press* for many years, was in Stan's history class, and evidently was a very bright student. He constantly asked questions, and Farmer later told his family that he, "Had to go home and study history every night to stay ahead of Lee."

At City, Stan was the line coach in football and assistant basketball coach under Yarnell Barnes. He also led the junior varsity to the City title in that division and took over the track squad in the spring.

He engaged in many activities at City including the experiment to allow boys to participate in Home Economics

Letterman's Club. Photo Courtesy of Central High.

while having the female students work in the Woodshop and Drafting. Unfortunately he did not develop a great talent for knitting and crocheting and serving. He and Coach Puckett were also advisors to the Letterman's Club.

The 1939 Dynamos described Coach Farmer as, "Having a winning personality and willingness to work that has made him an indisputable figure on the coaching staff."

Dynamo *tribute courtesy of City High*

Farmer participating in the Home Economics experiment.

Chapter V

Military Service

When World War II began, Stan's brother joined the Army and was stationed at Fort Oglethorpe. After talking to him, Stan decided to join the Navy. He travelled to Washington, D.C. hoping to enlist. However when he couldn't get past a receptionist at the Navy Department to see a recruiting officer, he went to Tennessee Congressman Estes Kefauver, who was a member of the House of Representatives from the 3rd Congressional District of Tennessee that included Chattanooga.

Kefauver took Stan back to the Navy office and after a discussion, he was allowed to enlist in the Navy in 1941 with the rank of Chief Petty Officer. Originally he trained recruits in San Diego until May 11, 1942, and later taught in Georgia in the flight school at the University of Georgia at Athens as a member of the staff for cadet training. He had enrolled in a special course for new officers at the U.S. Naval Academy in Annapolis, Maryland.

One potential hindrance to Stan enlisting in the Navy is that he suffered from "flat feet." He was told that if you rubbed dirt on your feet they wouldn't check very close and you would be approved for induction into the service. Rather than trying to get out of military service Stan Farmer was trying just the opposite – Serve his country.

His fellow soldiers loved Stan just like hjis athletes did. Photo courtesy of Farmer family.

Iwo Jima. Photo courtesy of Farmer family.

In February, 1942, he was selected for detachment to the Fifth Marine Division as Navy Gun Fire Officer. He was on active duty with the Marines in the battle of Saipan and Tinian, directing naval gunfire during the landings. Eventually he got tired of being in non-combat positions and volunteered for Army guard duty which involved placing naval gun crews aboard merchant vessels transporting arms and equipment to Europe. He was assigned guard duty on the tanker Sesso Portland on July 5, 1943.

During the historic battle of Iwo Jima in February-March, 1945, he was attached to the 26th Marines, landing with the Marines and coordinating and directing gunfire during the invasion. When Farmer observed that the driver of the Phillips landing craft was not planning to take his men all the way

Stan and buddies. Photo courtesy of Farmer family.

into the beach, he took affirmative action to ensure that his men would be placed safely on the beach. At Normandy and other amphibious landings, soldiers had died when dropped off in deep water with heavy equipment on their backs.

The pilot of his landing craft was apprehensive about their chances of landing safely. Farmer stiffened his resolve by placing his .45 caliber pistol against the back of the pilot's head and quietly informed the young man that "He did not want to get his feet wet." The craft safely landed and the Marines and Farmer disembarked.

While this method of persuasion may have been necessary in time of war, Farmer would use less drastic measures to motivate the thousands of young men in the future that he coached on the football field or taught in the classroom as a teacher and principal at Central High School from 1947-1978.

The hell that Stan Farmer and his fellow soldiers and Marines went through at Iwo Jima was reluctantly drawn out of him and related to his wife Katherine Farmer, daughter Kathy Farmer Ratz, and a few close friends. It was never done in a bragging or boastful manner but was in the tradition of servicemen (and women) who were reluctant to talk about their war time experiences. However there were some facts that were revealed and are repeated here to give the reader an insight as to what the troops endured during the Battle of Iwo Jima.

One of the most pleasant recollections by Stan Farmer was the day the flag was raised over Mount Suribachi when the mountain was finally scaled but the battle for the island

Photo reproduced from the original famous flag raising photograph signed and given to Stan Farmer. The photo was taken by Joe Rosenthal. Courtesy of Farmer family.

continued for several more weeks. He was given a signed copy of the flag raising photo made by photographer Joe Rosenthal, who took the picture and was involved in the controversy that surrounded the historical event.

After the American troops took control of the island, many Japanese soldiers remained hidden in the underground caves of Mount Suribachi and they were running out of food and water. To overcome their starvation they would crawl out of the caves at night to steal supplies from the U.S. troops.

Passwords were employed to keep the Japanese from shooting them at night and Navajo Indians were used as interpreters to convey orders and other information to each other because the Japanese could not understand the Navajo language.

According to Coach Farmer, the Americans dug their foxholes deep and he related that he could almost stand up in his. He remained in that crevice for eighteen days without coming out of it. No bathroom facilities were available and the only food they had to eat was chocolate candy in their rations.

Prior to landing on Iwo Jima, he had never smoked but developed the habit during that deadly battle which he continued for most of his life until his health deteriorated late in life and he had to quit at the insistence of his daughter, Kathy. Acquiring this wartime habit allowed him to overlook minor infractions of "no smoking" rules in his teaching capacity in later years.

Another little-known fact about Coach Farmer is an event during his naval career involving Ira Hayes, the Pima Indian, who was one of the Marines depicted in the famous statue raising of the flag over Mount Suribachi (Hot Rocks) at Iwo Jima. The memorial replica today stands at Arlington National Cemetery as a symbol honoring our nation's heroes.

Ira Hayes had difficulty adjusting to the hero status and adulation of the American public when he, and the other men made famous by the flag-raising, John Bradley, Ira Hayes, Franklin Sousley, Harlon Block, Rene Gagnon and Mike Strank were returned to the United States to participate in War Bond drives to raise money to help fund World War II.

Ira Hayes developed drinking problems that occurred on the tour. Ultimately, he was sent back to rejoin his unit, Easy Company, part of the 2nd Battalion, 28th Regiment of the Marine Corps. The stories about Ira's return to Easy Company are in conflict. One version was that his actions were an embarrassment to the military and the War Bond drive. The Marine Corps and the Bond Tour officials gave a different slant to the public in the news media. He was depicted as a soldier who wanted to return to combat and was being sent back to Company E "at his own request."

Ira Hayes in USMC servicde uniform. Photo courtesy of the National Archives for the United States Marine Corps.

After Ira returned to his unit, Coach Farmer was assigned to keep an eye on him. He stated that it was unfortunate that Ira was not strong enough to deal with the fame and notoriety of being depicted as a hero of Iwo Jima.

Coach Farmer learned of Ira's many concerns in conversations they had as they went through the various steps needed to return Ira to his unit where he felt more comfortable. Ira told Stan that it bothered him that adoring fans tore at his uniform and pulled at him. He also expressed a guilty conscience because of the fact that he was being honored while so many of his fellow soldiers in his company had died. Ira's life was depicted in a song "Battle of Ira Hayes" recorded in 1964 by Johnny Cash and which reached number three position on the Billboard Country Singles chart that year.

A movie on Ira's life, "The Outsider" was produced in 1961, with actor Tony Curtis in the role of Ira. Unfortunately it mostly depicted Ira's post-war experiences with alcohol which ultimately led to his death in the desert.

After coordinating and directing naval gunfire during the invasion at Sasebo, a core

Military commendation. Photo courtesy of Farmer family.

With his buddies. Photo courtesy of Farmer family.

Military medals. Courtesy of Farmer Family.

city in the Nagasaki Prefecture, Farmer was promoted to Lieutenant Commander in 1945 and assigned to Camp Lejeune, North Carolina.

Jeep named "Chattanooga Choo Choo." Photo courtesy of Farmer family.

After the United States dropped the two atomic bombs on Nagasaki and Hiroshima and the Japanese surrendered, Stan got into his "Chattanooga Choo Choo" Jeep and visited both sites without telling his commanding officers because he wanted to see for himself the terrible destruction. As a result military doctors for the rest of his life checked him for radiation.

In April, 1946, Farmer was made commanding officer of the Naval Detachment of the Amphibious Group at the Marine base. On August 15, 1946, he was ordered to inactive duty while at Camp Shelton, Norfolk, Virginia. He remained active in the Naval Reserves and was later commanding officer of Surface Division 6-76.

While serving in the Reserves and throughout his military career, he encouraged many of the less fortunate boys at

Another military commendation. Photo courtesy of the Farmer family.

Reunion of 5th Marine Division: John Alley, George E. Joyce, Stan Farmer, Henry Piasczky, and Brooke Pierce. Photo courtesy of Chattanooga Times Free Press.

Captured Japanese flag on Iwo Jima. Photo courtesy of Farmer family.

Yearly reunion of Iwo Jima Survivors in Chattanooga. Photo courtesy of Farmer family.

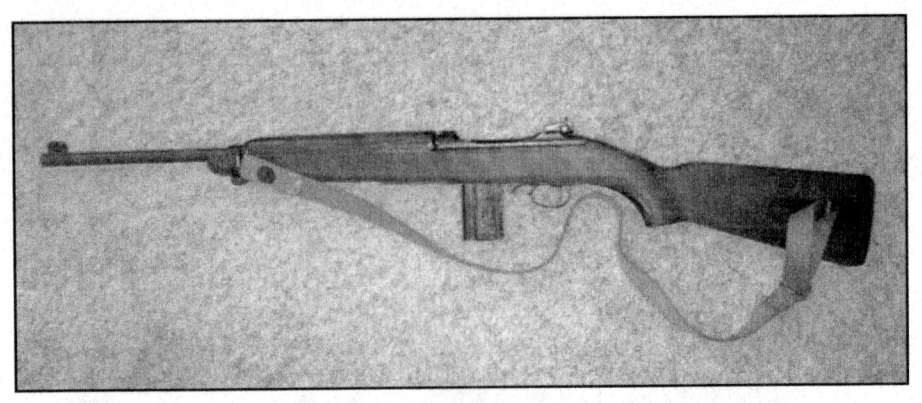

Stan's carbine. Photo courtesy Farmer family.

Central to join the reserves as a means of getting them some financial assistance due to their poor economic status.

For many years after the war, Stan and his surviving buddies from the Chattanooga area who served on Iwo Jima would have yearly reunions. The group included Jake Marshall, Duke Hicks, John Alley, Brooke Pierce, George E. Joyce, and Henry Piasczky.

Following his discharge from the Navy, Stan obtained employment with a fellow from Richmond, Virginia, that he met during the war who owned the Lehigh Portland Cement Plant and wanted to hire him as a salesman. Stan agreed to try the job for a year. He hated the position and said, "Those bricks would talk" to him.

When he was getting out of the service, he went to San Francisco and presented his carbine, his .45 caliber pistol, and his Japanese souvenirs to the Marine officer and was asked what unit he was attached to in the war. Stan replied "I'm in the Navy, attached to the 5th Marines."

The officer in charge stated they were not discharging Navy personnel, only Marines. As a result Stan backed out of

Kathy and her Japanese guest, Tokiwa Uchino. Photo by George Baker courtesy of Chattanooga Times.

the line and took his duffel bag which contained his contraband and went home.

After he had fulfilled his commitment, he eagerly accepted a job as assistant football coach on Coach E.B. "Red" Etter's staff for the 1947 season. Thus began a relationship with Central High School that would last until 1978.

Being a military veteran and survivor of the war in the Pacific, he initially had a hard feeling towards Japan and hated the little "sons of monkeys." He claimed that he dug the deepest foxhole on Iwo Jima and stated before he landed in the first wave on the beach that if anyone was going to get off the island, it was going to be him.

His attitude softened when his daughter, Kathy, hosted a Japanese exchange teacher. He became fond of her, and she translated the Japanese wording on the memorabilia that

Stan in uniform and in his dress whotes. Phtos courtesy of Farmer family.

he had brought home from the war. One day he told Kathy, "People don't make wars, governments do"

Stan Farmer loved his country. He proudly marched many times in Chattanooga's Armed Forces Day Parade.

A humorous event did occur on one parade march when Stan proudly wore his Navy Whites uniform. A torrential downpour arose, and he was not only seen proudly marching for the United States Navy, but the wet uniform also showed that he was proudly marching in his red polka dotted underwear.

Chapter VI

Central Coaching Career

1947-1969

1947

Stan Farmer was offered a coaching job when he ran into Central Principal Stacy Nelson at the barber shop in the old Masonic Building on Cherry Street in downtown Chattanooga in 1946. He asked to think about the offer and later called Mr. Nelson, accepting the job on the condition that he be allowed to finish out the one year commitment that he had made with the cement company in Virginia. The parties agreed, and former City High football great Stan Farmer became the football line coach at its long time arch rival, Central.

Hiring a graduate of City may have caused some apprehension by a small minority of the Central faithful, but Stan quickly dispelled their concerns with his enthusiasm and dedication to his job.

The 1947 coaching staff consisted of Head Football Coach E.B. "Red" Etter who had come to Central in 1942 after a suc-

Central Coaching Staff 1947, E.R. Etter, Jake Seaton, Les Newton, Stan Farmer. Photo courtesy of Central High.

cessful career at Brainerd Junior High, Lester Newton and Jake Seaton.

The origin of the term "Purple Pounders" is rumored to have come from the way that Central had overwhelmed a rival in a previous game. The original name of the team was the Central "Purples" and the addition of the term "Pounders" was added by an overenthusiastic *Times* sportswriter, Springer Gibson after a one sided victory in 1939.

Due to serious burn injuries to his legs that Coach Etter had sustained, he had been declared ineligible for military service during World War II. He would be recognized as one of the leading football coaches in Tennessee and the Southeast during his tenure at Central from 1942 until he retired in 1970. He compiled a record of over 200 wins with seven state championships. He also was an outstanding Latin and mathematics teacher and won two state championships in baseball. He served as boxing coach and initiated a wrestling program that eventually won several state championships.

During the summer he also coached the Post 14 American Legion baseball team, the Central Pennys, that was sponsored by local businessman and Central alumnus, Bill Penny, who operated Penny Tire and Marine on Dodds Avenue in East Chattanooga. This baseball team likewise achieved outstanding success under Coach Etter and several Purple Pounders signed minor league baseball contracts.

Coach Etter later taught and coached at Baylor School in Chattanooga and in 1973 won a mythical high school national championship with the Red Raiders. He would also continue his winning ways until he finally relinquished the coaching reins to his son, Gene. The younger Etter had graduated from Central in 1957 and played tailback for the University of Tennessee in their single wing offense. He would later play minor league baseball for nine years in the Chicago Cubs organization before retiring to become an assistant to his famed father at Baylor. He likewise would achieve an outstanding record as the baseball coach winning several state titles at that school in forty-one (41) years.

In addition to Coach Etter and Coach Farmer, two other important assistant coaches were Coaches Newton and Seaton. The four man coaching staff that would lead Central to many victories and several state championships was complete.

Les Newton graduated from Carson Newman College in 1930 and was the principal at Falling Water Grammar School before resigning to come to Central in 1941 to teach general science. He and Stan Farmer would jointly coach the Central linemen that would be a major factor in the Pounders gridiron success.

Stanly J. Farmer: We Called Him Coach
~ 52 ~

First Row-Left to Right: E. Grizzle, E. Easy, M. Carroll, J.E. Vick, J. Foust, G. Tate, B. McKenzie, D. Jackson, P. Fuller, D. Sanders, R. Allison
Second Row-Left to Right: Mgr. Bremer, K. Baress, B. Bradford, B. Crawford, D. Hawkins, L. Winters, Capt. Allison
Third Row-Left to Right: Coach Newton, Mgr. R. Porter, C. Walker, J. Snider, E. Kelley, O. Anderson, R. Belcin, G. Sexton, R. Miller, D. Westbrook, J. Ss, A. Kimberg, C. McCurdy, C. Hall, I. Allison, L. Ma Benett, Mgr. Sanderson
Fourth Row-Left to Right: D. Gordon, J. Smith, T. Wilkens, D. Smith, T. Wilkens, I. Neal, D. Smith, T. Wilkens, I. McKamen, T. Bryan, B. Tate, D. Redding, E. Derrick

Central 26 Lafayette 6
Central 21 Tyner 0
Central 19 Young 7
Central 0 B___ 7
Central 13 Red Bank 2
Central 7 Knoxville City 26
Central 0 Mule Hgh 13
Central 0 ____ ___
Central 0 Easley 0
Central 0 Bayor 19
Central 0 Oak Ridge 6
Central 21 city 6

1947 Purple Pouders squad. Photo courtesy of Central High

J.M. "Boots" Seaton, a graduate from East Tennessee State University, was in charge of the "B" team which helped develop many younger players to prepare them to later play on the varsity squad. Seaton's method of coaching was to toughen up the players by a lot of blocking and tackling exercises such as "bull in the pen" where the players would form a circle. A player inside the circle would be given the ball and try to bust through the circle. Many varsity players would credit Coach Seaton with toughening them up to prepare for varsity squad play. Seaton taught industrial arts and had tremendous strength in his hands. Many students who challenged him in a grip contest would learn that Coach Seaton could quickly put the younger student on the ground in a friendly contest.

Coach Farmer was described as having a "friendly, genial manner, and pleasing personality that had won the admiration of the Central students."

Guard J.T. Vick selected for the Chattanooga Times All-City Team. Photo courtesy of Central High.

Lamar Wheat, Georgia Tech All American, Central Sports Hall of Fame. Photo courtesy of Central High.

The forty-two member squad achieved a record of 6-5-1 which was climaxed by a 41-6 victory over arch rivalry City High Dynamos.

Captain and tackle Lamar Wheat and guard J.T. Vick won recognition by being selected for the *Chattanooga Times* All-City Team in 1947. Lamar Wheat would win a scholarship to Georgia Tech and would become an All American tackle for the Rambling Wrecks. Wheat would also be selected as a member of the inaugural Athletic Hall of Fame Class at Central in 2013. In addition to his teaching and coaching duties Stan was the school sponsor for the all-female Trail Trotters Club.

1948

The Purple Pounders record on the gridiron was 6-6-1 in 1948. For the first time Coach Farmer was given the nickname "Boomer." The origin of the moniker is unknown but two alternative theories exist. One is that he earned the designation by his loud voice while a second theory is that it was based on his prosperity to not so gently place his foot on the rear end of one of his down linemen when they were not performing up to his expectations.

In addition to his coaching duties Farmer was a member of the physical education department of Central.

Starring players on the 1948 Purple Pounder squad were "Lightning" Leon Henry and captain J.T. Vick, who both earned Second All-City Team honors at guard along with halfback Johnny Bach.

Halfback John Childers and tackle Dorsey Gardner were selected as members of the First All-City Team selected by the *Chattanooga Times.*

Coach Farmer demonstrated his ability as a recruiter of outstanding players when he convinced end Norman Hofferman to come to Central rather than attend arch rival City High.

By tradition most Jewish players attended City but Coach Farmer at the request of Bucky Shamberger convinced Norman and his mother so he could go to the school on Dodds Avenue. Due to the unique situation, Coach Etter addressed the football team and asked what their feel-

1948 Purple Pounders squad. Photo courtesy of Central Hi8gh.

1948 Purple Pouders. Photo courtesy of Central High.

1948 Captain J. T. Vick, left, and End Norman Hofferman, right. Photos courtesy of Central High.

ings were about a Jewish person playing for Central. By a unanimous vote he was welcomed to the team and became a starter in three sports and was offered a scholarship to Georgia Tech. He could not accept the offer because of his religious prohibition on Saturday football play.

However his greatness was recognized by the Jewish Community Center in Chattanooga, being selected for its Regional Sports Hall of Fame. In 2015 he was installed as a member of the Central High Sports Hall of Fame.

An interesting corollary to the Norman Hofferman story is that when he came home proudly wearing his first Central purple "C" sweater his mother stated that she didn't know why he was so eager to play football since he was only good enough to earn a "C" grade in the sport.

Stanly J. Farmer: We Called Him Coach
~ 58 ~

1949

Central	46	Tyner	7
Central	7	Knox Young	14
Central	2	Kingsport	20
Central	6	Red Bank	0
Central	51	Oak Ridge	13
Central	18	Miami	19
Central	40	Rossville	12
Central	14	Bradley	0
Central	14	Baylor	7
Central	41	City	6

1949 Purple Pounders squad. Photo courtesy of Central High

1949

The 1949 season gave an indication of better things to come in the future for the Purple Pounders as the team acquired a record of 7 wins against only 3 losses. Winning their last four games that included a victory over Baylor (14-7) and the season finale against City High (41-6) before a crowd of over 15,000 fans on the Friday after Thanksgiving was impressive.

Pounder captain and future assistant coach Bill Tate scored one of the touchdowns on a pass from quarterback Bucky Shamberger. Another future assistant football and head baseball coach Jimmy Hale was a halfback on the squad. Hale would coach the 1960 Purple Pounders to a state championship in baseball.

Many members of the team earned all-star honors. Central was awarded the City Championship trophy and Bill McKenzie, Jim Allison, and Johnny Back were selected on the *Chattanooga News-Free Press* All-City Team and Bill McKenzie, Bucky Shamberger, and Dickie Sanders were picked for the *Chattanooga Times* All-City squad. However the highest honors would go to lineman

1949 Captain Bill Tate. Photo courtesy of Central High.

Bill McKenzie who was selected to the All-Southern Eastern Division and honorable mention high school All American.

Coach Farmer was carried off the field on the shoulders of Pounder players after the City victory.

Victory over City. Photo courtesy of Central High.

1950

The 1950 Purple Pounder squad had a record of 8-2-1 with the losses coming to Knoxville Young (19-12), Baylor (21-6), and a tie (7-7) with the Miami Central Stingarees before a crowd of 10,000 at Chamberlain Field, home of the University of Chattanooga Moccasins.

"Lightning" Leon Henry had an outstanding senior year and Norman Hofferman, Jimmy Hale, and Bucky Shamberger were just a few of the players who made significant contributions to the team's success. Newcomers Jimmy Pack and ninth grade sensation Bobby Hoppe gave a preview during the season of things to come for the Purple Pounders.

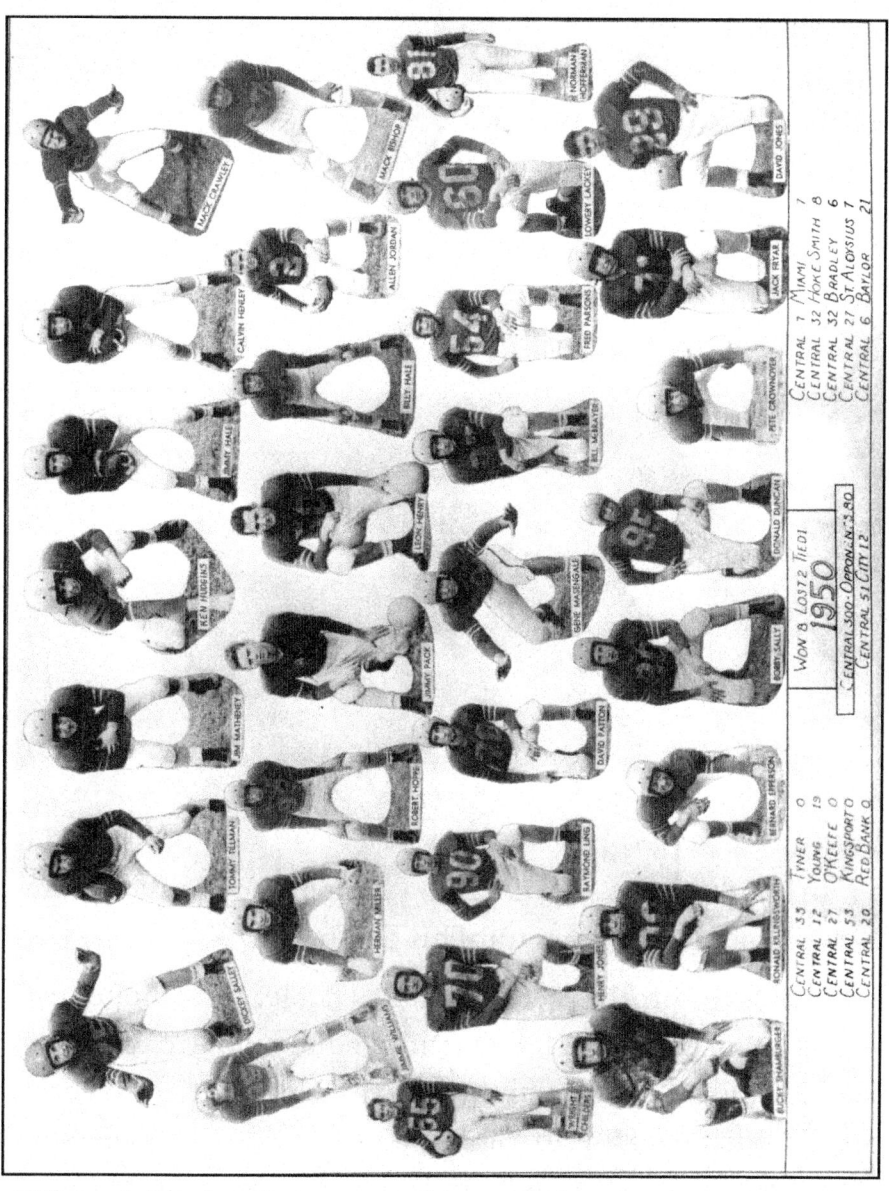

1950 Purple Pounders. Photo courtesy of Central High

Wedding day 1950. Photo courtesy of Farmer family.

In 1950 Stan wed Katherine Phillips who would become his soulmate for 46 years until his death in 1996.

The Sally brothers, Bobby and Dickie, were hopeful of getting scholarships to further their education. Coach Farmer and Katherine took the boys to the University of Georgia to see Coach Wally Butts about getting them a scholarship. They received grant-in-aid's and over the objection of Coach

Farmer their father bought them a car. As the result they both flunked out of school.

Katherine was a graduate of Marion County High School and the Andrew Jackson Business College in Nashville. She was employed at Davidson Department Store in Chattanooga when she first met Stan Farmer. Stan was working at a nearby men's store as a summer employee. The observant Katherine noticed that several women were seen visiting him during work hours but she managed to beat the competition after they met in 1948.

In 1955 she gave birth to their only child, Kathy Farmer (Ratz) who was the proverbial apple of her daddy's eye. She graduated from Central and Middle Tennessee State University in special education, trained in the instruction of deaf and blind students teaching them braille.

Arrival of Daddy's girl, Kathy. Photo courtesy of Farmer family.

The daughter grows up. Courtesy of Farmer family.

Red Bank graduate Gordon Atchley was added as another assistant coach after graduation from the University of Chattanooga where he played end on the football team. His playing experience at that position in college led to a significant improvement in the performance of Central ends

1951

Central was awarded its first mythical state championship by Vanderbilt professor E.E. Litkenhous with the team's record of 10 wins and only 1 loss to the Miami Central team by a score of 14-12. The game played in Miami was the first airplane trip for most of the Pounder squad and several of the coaching staff.

The emergence of Jimmy Pack at quarterback and the continued development of Bobby Hoppe as running and defensive back led the offensive efforts of the Purple Pounders. Aggressive line play under the direction of Coaches Farmer and Newton made it difficult for opposing teams to cross

Coaching staff 1951: Newton, Farmer, Etter, Seaton, Atchley. Courtesy of Central High

the goal line on Central. Eight opposing squads on the schedule were held to either seven points or shut out completely by the aggressive defensive unit.

Bobby Hoppe would become part of the Farmer legend when he viciously tackled an opposing player and sustained the loss of several teeth. He recovered them, went to the sidelines, handed his teeth to Coach Farmer, and requested that he hold them and went back into the game.

First State Championship, 1951. Photo courtesy of Central High.

1952

Coach Etter introduced the T formation in 1952 as the Purple Pounders were chosen Tennessee State Champions for the second consecutive season by the Associated Press.

The team won all of its games against Tennessee opponents and the only blemishes on the record was a one-point loss to Miami Central (19-18) and a tie with the Kentucky State Champions Louisville Flaget (7-7). The Pounders dominated the post season all-star teams with quarterback Jimmy Pack being chosen for the All-Southern Team. Guard Don Duncan, Pack and Bobby Hoppe were selected on the All-State first team while end Dan Wade was picked for the second team.

Guard Don Duncan and halfback Tommy Tillman were elected as captain and alternate captain of the 1952 team. Tillman later became a minister and missionary to the Far East

1952 Captains Don Duncan, left, and Tommy Tillman, right. Courtesy of Central High.

1952 State Champs. Photo courtesy of Central High.

where he was responsible for providing not only religion, but also medical treatment in several countries.

Duncan had an aunt who worked with Katherine and they argued every day. She was a member of the Church of God religion and believed that it was a sin to play sports and unfortunately none of his family ever saw him play. He was later offered a coaching job at City and McCallie. He stated that in his opinion, "Central kids loved each other and City kids loved themselves."

Central was playing in Jacksonville, Florida, and the team stayed at a hotel on the beach. After bed check Stan heard noises on the beach and he and Coach Seaton went to check, along with the hotel manager. They found player Sherwin Anderson out cold from swimming in the icy water. The manager said that Sherwin needed some whiskey to be poured down him in order to bring him around. Stan told the manager that he wouldn't do that, but the manager did give Sherwin the whiskey and he recovered.

Fullback Banjie Geren lived in Glenwood and would often go home for lunch between the morning and afternoon practice sessions in August. Although the players had been warned about eating light, his mother on one occasion fixed a big meal that included steak and all the trimmings.

Banjie went back to practice, then threw up most of the afternoon. Coach Farmer told him, "Next time maybe you will listen to me." Banjie sheepishly told Stan, "I'm going to tell my mother on you." Stan reported that he should also tell her, "I had kicked his fanny."

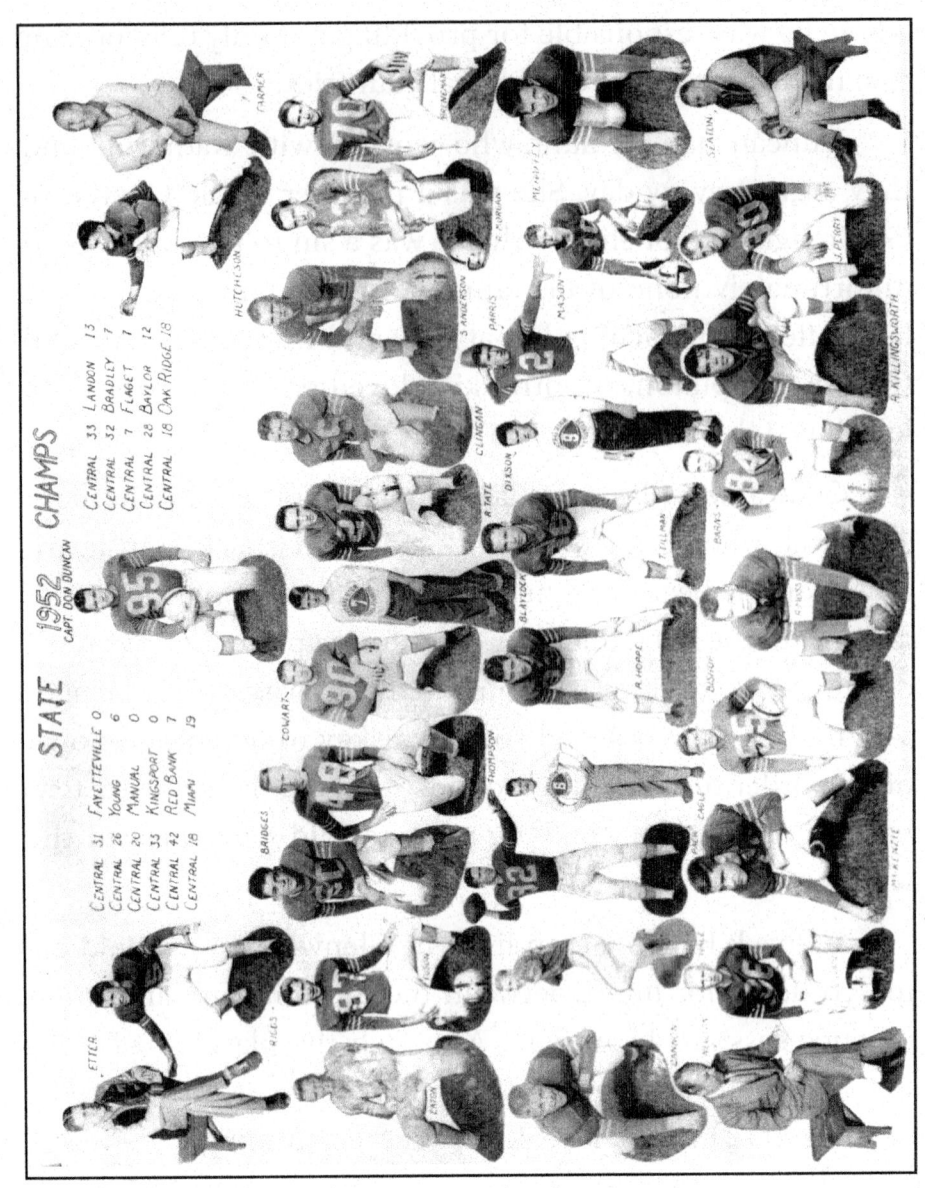

1952 State Champs. Photo courtesy of Central High.

1953

Vanderbilt Professor E.E. Litkenhous recognized Central as the 1953 Tennessee State Champions based on his complicated mathematical formula that ranked the high school football teams in Tennessee.

The season opening game did not indicate that they would repeat as state champions as the Pounders lost to Memphis Central by a score of 16-7 before 12,000 spectators at Chamberlain Field.

Playing an intersectional schedule that included games with Memphis Central, Atlanta Marist, Kingsport Dobyns - Bennett, Miami Central, Jacksonville Landon, Bradley County, and Nashville Litton, the Pounders compiled a record of nine wins, one loss, and a tie with Bradley County. The Miami team came to Chamberlain Field on October 9 and the Pounders prevailed 27-0 for its first win in 6 games against the South Floridians.

The team travelled to Miami for a second game with the Stingarees and prevailed 21-14 before a crowd of 18,479 fans in the Little Orange Bowl game on December 11.

The squad was led by Captain Bobby Hoppe who earned All-City, All-State, All Southern, and All American honors as one of the greatest backs to come out of the Chattanooga area. He would later play for Auburn University and in the National Football League. Hoppe was selected posthumously in the initial Central Athletic Hall of Fame in 2013. After Bobby Hoppe had scored several touchdowns in one of the Miami

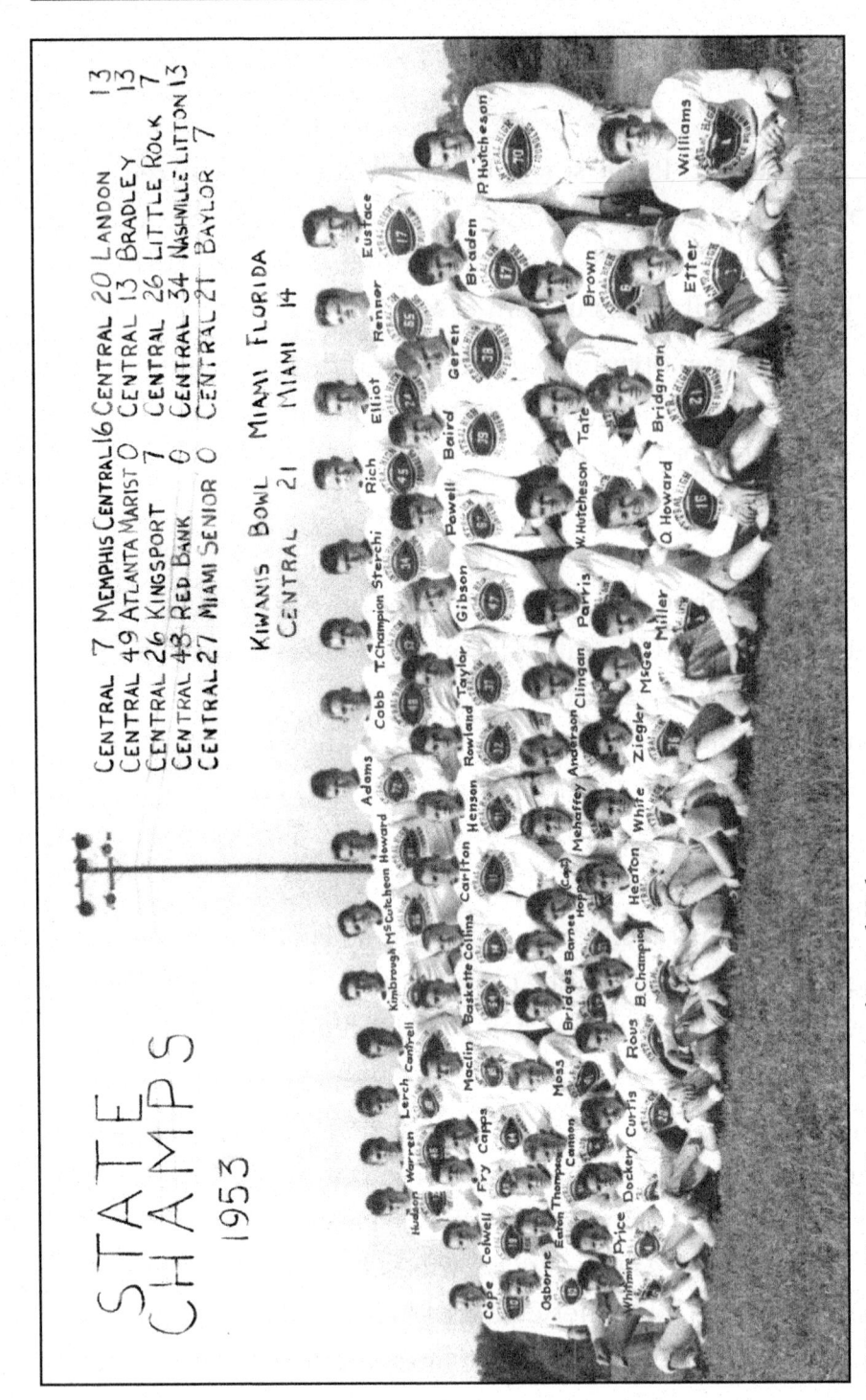

1953 State Champs. Photo courtesy of Central High

games, he was breathing hard and encountered Coach Farmer. Stan told Bobby, "If you hadn't been smoking cigarettes you would have scored several more."

One incident that started out serious but turned humorous occurred when an ad appeared in the football program which showed a picture of Coach Farmer with the exclamation, "Joy and I enjoy eating at Beathea's Restaurant." Katherine at first didn't think the ad was funny but after it was explained that it was a mistake, she also enjoyed a good laugh.

Bobby Hoppe in 1953., Central's greatest back, Phto courtesy of Central High

During the 1953 season seven Pounders were picked on the All-City team. Hoppe, fullback Wayne Hutcheson, end James Cannon, guard Hal Bridges, tackle Larry Clingan, tackle Richard Cowart, and center Ray Moss were all honored. With five of the seven being linemen, the teaching and influence of Coach Farmer in getting the best out of the young men who toiled in the trenches for Central was evident. Nine other members of the team received Honorable Mention designations. Hoppe and Bridges were chosen as Tennessee All-State players.

"B" team Coach "Boots" Seaton was joined by Coach Charlie Farmer as the Pounders continued to build a dynasty from the ground up.

One of the few areas in which Coach Etter and Coach Farmer differed was in dealing with Bobby Hoppe. Coach Farmer contended that when Hoppe was scoring touchdowns, he was Coach Etter's boy. But when he would pull

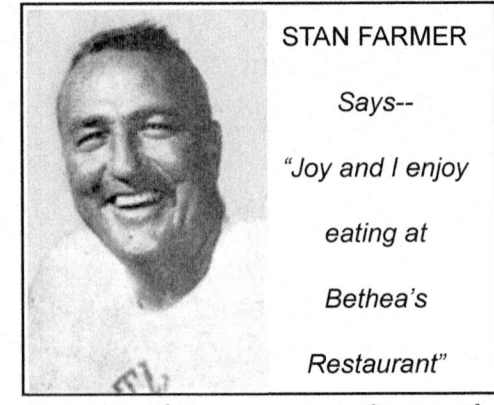

STAN FARMER

Says--

"Joy and I enjoy eating at Bethea's Restaurant"

Erroneous ad in game program. Courtesy of Central High.

Principal Hobart Millsap, coaches, and players get ready to fly to Miami to play in the Little Orange Bowl. Photo courtesy of Central High.

stunts such as breaking all of the commode lids in the boys bathroom he was Coach Farmer's boy. Coach Farmer also believed that Coach Etter sometime punished different players unequally when they got in trouble for the same offense.

Coach Farmer described that he would handle the problems and not tell Coach Etter about disciplining all boys equally and this worked well while they were coaching together.

1953 Captains: Al McHaffey, Bobby Hoppe, Neil Barnes. Photo courtesy Central High.

1953 Coaching Staff: S. Farmer, Newson, Etter, Seaton, C. Farmer. Photo courtesy of Central High.

Another Hoppe caper was when the team played in Florida and the team stayed at a motel that didn't have a restaurant. When the coaches and bus driver, Red Brown, went deep sea fishing, Red left the keys to the bus in the ignition. The boys loaded up the bus and Hoppe drove them to a restaurant to get something to eat.

1954

In spite of a one-point loss to Memphis Central (14-13), the squad was once again selected as Tennessee's finest football team in 1954 with a record of 10 wins versus 1 loss.

The Pounder coaching staff of Etter, Farmer, Newton, and Seaton had completed forty three cumulative seasons of teaching young men on the gridiron.

Led by All-City, All-State, All Southern, and All America alternate captain Ray Moss, and All-City and All-State Captain Larry Clingan, Central, once again dominated the all-star selections.

In addition to these honors, Moss was selected as Lineman of the Year in the Tri-State area. He would be awarded a scholarship to the University of Tennessee and played briefly with the Buffalo Bills in the American Football League. He and father, Ray Moss, Sr. and brother-in-law, Lyle Finley, would start the highly successful Milk Jug-Golden Gallon convenience stores. Moss unfortunately would die in a plane crash two days short of his fortieth birthday and Central lost one of its most dedicated graduates. After Central moved to

Jerry H. Summers
~ 77 ~

1954 State Champs. Photo courtesy of Central High.

1954 Squad. Photo courtesy of Central High.

1954 Captains Ray Moss, Jr., left, and Larry Clingan, right. Courtesy of Central High.

the Highway 58 location in 1969, Moss headed a committee of alumni who raised the money to build Central War Memorial Stadium/Etter-Farmer Field without any Hamilton County Board of Education financial support. Moss was selected as a member of the initial Central Sports Hall of Fame in 2013. Clingan would also become successful in his family's' heating and air conditioning business and supported Central until his death.

Former 1951 Central graduate Jimmy Hale joined the coaching staff after attending Western Kentucky University and began teaching history in the fall of 1954.

This was the year that the concrete stands at Frawley Field on McCallie Avenue were being torn down and steel spikes were lying around everywhere. Jim Maclin, a Central player, fell and a spike went into one of his lungs. Coach Farmer was summoned, stopped the blood flow by putting his hand over the puncture, and Jim was transported to a local hospital where fortunately he recovered fully.

1954 Central coaching staff: Les Newton, Bill Tate, Jimmy Hale, Jake Seaton, E. B. Etter, Stanley Farmer. Photo courtesy of Central High.

1955

The string of four consecutive state championships came to an end as the Pounders fell to a record of seven wins versus three losses. The three close losses came in games against Memphis Central (12-6), Kingsport (20-12), and Baylor (18-7).

The team made its first of several bowl game trips to Jacksonville, Florida, to play in the Meninak Bowl, a charity game that would put Central against the outstanding teams in the Florida city.

Led by future Auburn University fullback Ronnie Robbs and later United States Military Academy graduate quarterback Bobby Rudesill, the Pounders came close to a fifth consecutive state championship but fell short.

Central, in the Portland game, lost the talents of running back Charles Cantrell to a serious knee injury when he was tackled out of bounds and struck a yard marker on the sidelines. Cantrell weighed 225 pounds and was extremely fast. He was one of the few backs to play at Central to be compared to the legendary Bobby Hoppe. Cantrell had some character flaws that often put him under the strict discipline skills of Coach Farmer.

Cantrell came from a poor economic background. One August, Coach Farmer and Katherine went to the player's East Lake home because Charlie and his family did not have any food. The next day Coach Farmer got in touch with Ray Moss's father who promised to leave milk at their house as long as

1955 Pounders. Photo courtesy of Central High.

Charlie played at Central. He also contacted another player's (Charlie Cobb) father, who gave Charles' mother a job in his laundromat.

Cantrell was a constant discipline problem and the Farmers often had to go to his house. He had been seen smoking a cigar in the hall and Stan decided to take Coach Etter with him to talk to his mother. When Coach Etter told Charlie's mother of the incident, she told the respected coach, "Why didn't you knock the G.D. cigar out of his mouth?" and Coach Etter, being a strong Christian couldn't reply and left.

The efforts of Coach Farmer and his wife Katherine to help

Jerry H. Summers
~ 83 ~

1955 Lettermen. Photo courtesy of Central High.

Charles are well-known to the surviving players of that era. Charles' stay at Central resulted in many acts of misconduct, but he possessed as much natural talent as anyone who ever played for Central until it was all lost when he sustained a serious career-ending injury in the Portland game in 1955.

1955 was also the year that the Farmers were expecting their first child. Katherine was having a lot of problems, and the doctor said that she might not be able to carry the child full term. She had to stay in bed for a couple of months. Although Stan promised to keep her condition quiet, he told the team at football practice and they gave her a baby shower at the Larry Clingan's family house on the lake to demonstrate their love and respect for the Farmers. They were given a lot of nice gifts including a gold locket by Ray Moss, Jr.

Led by All-City and All-State Captain guard Paul Hutcheson and alternate captain Bobby Baskette, the Pounders enjoyed a winning season that might have been better without the injury to Cantrell.

Charles Cantrell in action. Photo courtesy of Central High.

1955 Captains Paul Hutcheson. left, and Bobby Baskette, right. Photos courtesy of Central High.

Bill Tate, left, and Jimmy Hale, right, assistant coaches.

Several seniors signed grant-in-aid to southern schools. Fullback Ronnie Robbs and Rudesill both signed with Auburn University; quarterback Rudesill would eventually go to Army. Guard Paul Hutcheson signed with Georgia Tech, end Bobby Baskette with Alabama and halfback Paul Elliot with Georgia.

Baskette would be a hero in baseball as he drove in the winning run in one of Central's two consecutive state championships under Coach Etter during this era.

Former Central players, end Bill Tate and running back Jimmy Hale, joined the coaching staff as assistant coaches.

1956

What hopefully would return the Pounders to competing for a state championship in 1956 turned out to be Coach Etter's only losing season during his tenure at Central. With a severe knee injury to Captain and star running back Benny Parks, the team was only able to attain a record of four wins, five losses, and two ties. Close losses to Memphis Southside (13-10), Birmingham Woodlawn (20-12), Knoxville Fulton (20-14), and Jacksonville Lee (7-6) in the Meninak Bowl combined with ties with Memphis Central (7-7) and Kingsport (7-7) prevented another outstanding record.

Gene Etter completed his sixth season as placekicker for the Pounders and was awarded a scholarship to the University of Tennessee, where he was an outstanding single wing tailback and baseball player.

Jerry H. Summers
~ 87 ~

1956 Captains Lonnie Styles, Bennier Parks, and Jimmy Henley. Photo courtesy of Central High.

Wingman, All American, Ronnie Kincer. Photo courtesy of Central High.

Gene Etter. Courtesy of University of Tennessee Athletic Department

Gene Etter., Central Sports Hall of Fame. Courtesy of Central High.

Stanly J. Farmer: We Called Him Coach
~ 88 ~

1956

1956 Pounders squad. Photo courtesy of Central High.

Gene would also be selected as a member of the inaugural class of the Central Sports Hall of Fame in 2013. In addition to Benny Parks serving as captain of the team, center Jimmy Henley and guard Lonnie Styles were alternate captains for the year.

Unfortunately several members of the team engaged in some misconduct during the Meninak Bowl which may have contributed to the loss to Robert E. Lee squad when the holder for the extra point to tie the game fumbled the ball.

When the misconduct was discovered after the game, Coach Farmer was assigned to the task of rounding up the wrongdoers. While searching one of the rooms he found a

The Weasel, Terrill Garrison, center, and managers, left to right, Jackie Pritchard, Tommy Acklen, Richard Helton and Johnny McCoy. Courtesy of Central High.

member of the managerial staff hiding under the bed and said to him, "You little weasel, come out of there." A lifetime nickname was applied to one of the most loyal Pounder supporters which followed the young man until his death in 2015.

Guard Ronnie Kincer was selected as an All-State player and would attend college in Louisiana. He would also be chosen as a high school All-American by Wigwam Wisemen of America. He also drove in the winning run when Central won the state baseball title in 1956.

One humorous incident concerning Coach Farmer occurred at the new Central practice field in Glenwood after it opened in the fall of 1956. Yellow jackets got up in the shorts that he wore at practice and he had to shed them quickly. As he normally did not wear undershorts, the sight of him baring his anatomy to avoid any stings produced a memorable event for the football team.

Another incident occurred at the Glenwood facility when a young man was hiding in the woods and was shooting Coach Farmer in the back with a BB gun. He chased the boy, took away his rifle and locked it up in his car. Katherine made him return the gun and the young man got off with a warning that if it ever happened again, the police would be called.

1957

Prospects for a winning season did not look bright for the Pounders in 1957 with only one returning starter from the previous year.

However winning several games by close scores, the squad was able to finish the regular season undefeated with ten victories. Unfortunately the chance for a perfect season during the Etter-Farmer era was marred by a loss to Jacksonville Robert E. Lee (14-0) in the season-ending Meninak Bowl.

Central was selected by E.E. Litkenhous as state champions. The highlight of the season was the 8-0 win over the Oak Ridge Wildcats at Chamberlain Field in a downpour. A punt by quarterback Chink Brown floated out of bounds on the one

1957 Captains, Chink Brown, Eddie Lance, Jimmy Cheek. Courtesy of Central High.

1957 State Champs. Photo courtesy of Central High.

yard line which backed Oak Ridge up to its goal line in the final minutes of the game.

Quarterback Chink Brown, center and linebacker Eddie Lance and defensive halfback Jimmy Cheek served as captains for the team. Chink Brown and Eddie Lance were both selected for the All-City and All-State teams and were awarded scholarships to Auburn University. Halfback James "Happy" Mallet and junior guard Buddy Hale were named to the second team All-City team. Lance was later named a High School All-American by a national publication.

One of the other big victories for the year was a 29-12 win over Scottsboro, Alabama, which was led by All-State quarterback Pat Trammell. He would be the starter for Alabama Coach Paul "Bear" Bryant when the Crimson Tide won the National Championship in 1960. Halfback James "Happy" Mallett was the outstanding performer in that game.

1958

If prospects for the 1957 team seemed weak at the beginning of the season, they appeared even less exciting for 1958. Several players rose to the occasion and the team compiled a record of ten wins and one loss. The one loss was a replay of the 1957 state championship game with Oak Ridge. Before a crowd of 10,000 spectators in Oak Ridge, the Wildcats, led by tailback Jackie Pope, defeated the Purple Pounders by a score of 14-6.

Central 21 Johnson City 0	Central 27 Nashville Hillsboro 0
Central 26 Memphis Humes 14	Central 59 Scottsboro 0
Central 26 Memphis Central 7	Central 6 Oak Ridge 14
Central 20 Kingsport 0	Central 37 Memphis Southside 13
Central 14 Bradley 7	Central 21 Robert E. Lee 7

1958

1958 State Runnerup. Photo courtesy of Central High.

1958 Captains: Terrell Dye, Grady Wade, and Buddy Hale. Courtesy of Central High.

End Grady Wade and tackle Paul "Bull" Chapman were both selected to the first-team All-State squad and were also All-City first team honorees. Tackle Bobby Locke was placed on the All-State second team and center George Shuford and halfback Terrell Dye were placed on the third team.

Wade, Chapman, Locke, and Dye were chosen for the All-City first team with Hale and Shuford picked for the All-City second team. Junior fullback Gilbert Trusley and end Buddy Norton were picked for the All-City third team and others made Honorable Mention.

Wade and Dye would sign grants-in-aid to Vanderbilt University. Shuford would attend the University of Tennessee at Knoxville and would become a kicker who established the record for the longest field goal of 53 yards. He also would be selected as the catcher on the Volunteers All-Time baseball team. He entered the Central Sports Hall of Fame in 2013.

Shuford almost quit football as a sophomore when it became apparent that he wasn't going to make the starting team at fullback, a position he had played in junior high. Coach Farmer convinced George to return to the team and he was moved to center in 1957, backing up Eddie Lance. In 1958 he would be the starter at both center and linebacker.

Bobby Locke, left and George Shuford, right. Photos courtesy of Central High.

Of the players on the starting offense, ten would receive some offer of an athletic scholarship. In addition to eight football players, Butch Harless wrestled for the University of Chattanooga and Jerry Summers played baseball at Auburn University and attended Sewanee to play basketball and baseball. Alternate captain Grady Wade and captain Terrell Dye received grants-in-aid to Vanderbilt, Buddy Hale to Auburn, Robert Kelly and Buddy Norton to Austin Peay, and Mike O'Brien to the University of Chattanooga.

1959

With only captain Paul Chapman returning at tackle and alternate captain Gilbert Trusley coming back at fullback, the sixteenth season under the leadership of Coach Etter and the twelfth season for Coach Farmer, the prospects once again did not seem high for the 1959 Purple Pounders. The season lived up to those expectations as the team finished with a record of 5 wins, four losses, and a tie.

Trusley would eventually win a football scholarship to the University of Tennessee and quarterback Wayne Haling and safety Bert Brown would earn baseball scholarships for their performances on the 1960 Pounder state championship squad.

1959 Captains, Gilbert Trusley and Paul Chapman. Photo courtesy of Central High.

In the last game of the long-running practice of closing the season in the Meninak Bowl in Jacksonville, the Pounders lost to the Robert E. Lee Generals (19-7).

In the spring of 1960 Coach Farmer was offered a job at Peerless Woolen Mills in Rossville, Georgia, as personnel director by Bob McCoy, former Central football player and member of the inaugural Central Sports Hall of Fame. It was a much better paying job

1959 Pounders squad. Photo courtesy of Central High.

Bob McCoy, Central Sports Hall of Fame. Courtesy of Central High.

than what coaches and teachers earned in education. He resigned at the end of the school year and worked that summer at the plant.

But as football season came around, Coach Farmer had second thoughts and went back to Central. Later he would describe his business experience as, "My summer job." He told his family that he didn't enjoy firing "old people."

Obviously Coach Etter was overjoyed to have Farmer back as his aide, and they enjoyed many more years producing winning teams for Central before Etter's retirement to go to Baylor School.

It has been rumored that Coach Etter wanted Coach Farmer to go with him to Baylor when he retired in 1969, but Coach Farmer decided to remain faithful to Central and fill out his remaining years in education as athletic director and assistant principal.

1960 Captains, Benny Hartman, left, and Aaron Watt, right. Photos courtesy of Central High.

1960

Central 12	Johnson City 0	Central 28 Huntsville Butler 7
Central 23	Memphis Central 0	Central 20 Red Bank 0
Central 0	Etowah County 13	Central 6 Greenwood, S.C. 16
Central 6	Kingsport 13	Central 20 Oak Ridge 33
Central 7	Bradley 14	Central 33 Knoxville Young 0

1960 Pounders squad. Photo courtesy of Central High.

Coching staff 1960: Farmer, Etter, Archer, Hale and Seaton

1960

While achieving only a 5 win – 5 loss season, the 1960 Central team was ranked fourth in the Litkenhous rating because of its strong performances against state champion Kingsport and runner-up Bradley County, losing by only a touchdown in each game. Each of the other losses were close and Central with a little bit of luck could have had a much better record. The Kingsport loss was particularly hard as the Indians scored the winning touchdown with only twenty-five seconds remaining on the clock. The team, which was captained by fullback Benny Hartman and backed up by halfback alternate captain Aaron Watts, was a much better team than its record indicated.

1961

1961 Pounder squad. Photo courtesy of Central High.

A new addition to the coaching staff was former Ohio State and University of Chattanooga halfback Jack Archer who would work with Coach Etter instructing the backs.

Stan and Katherine continued their recruiting ways as they encouraged sophomore halfback Steve Bevil to attend Central rather than City High. Steve originally told Coach Farmer he was going to City but after Katherine talked to Steve's dad, he changed his mind and enrolled at Central. He later would earn a scholarship to Vanderbilt University after the 1962 state championship season. Quarterback Jerry Shuford would also earn a grant-in-aid to Vanderbilt in 1960.

1961

In spite of a record of eight wins and only two losses, one to State Champion Bradley County by a score of 13-7, the Pounders only could finish seventh in the Litkenhous ratings. A lopsided loss to Oak Ridge late in the season by a score of 26-7 may have caused the reduced standings position.

Captains 1961 Tammy Aiken and Dickie Byrns. Photo courtesy of Central high.

With a multitude of returning players, the coaching staff and players looked forward to an outstanding 1962 season.

Captains Tommy Aiken and Dickie Byres provided excellent team leadership as the team finished another successful season under Coach Etter and Coach Farmer and their staff.

A 7-6 win over the top-ranked Kingsport was probably the most exciting game of the season. However, the continued dominance of the Pounders over Coach Farmer's *alma mater*, City High (21-8) would have to be another highlight.

1962

As expected the 1962 Central football season started with high anticipation for a successful year. Central alumni and fans were not disappointed as the Pounders executed well enough to go undefeated in 11 games.

Beginning with its fifth victory in a row over Johnson City (14-0) and ending with the season finale win in the Meninak Bowl in Jacksonville, Florida, over Robert E. Lee (28-12), the Pounders displayed both a potent offense and tough defense to accomplish the first undefeated season in Central history and Coach E.B. Etter and Coach Stan Farmer's careers.

Many members of the squad received post-season recognition. They were led by tackle Dickie Phillips, who received the Thom McAnn Award given each year to the Best Player in the area. He was also voted the Best Blocker and Most Outstanding Player on the Central team. Other honors garnered by Phillips were selections to the All-City, All-State,

1962 State Champs. Photo courtesy of Central High.

1962 Captains, Dickie Phillips and Scott Campbill. Photo courtesy of Central High.

All Southern, and All-American teams. He would receive a grant-in-aid to the University of Georgia where he would play defensive tackle for the Bulldogs. Phillips would also be voted into the Central High Athletic Hall of Fame in 2014. His brother, quarterback Harry Phillips, would also win a scholarship to Georgia.

Halfbacks Steve Bevil and Terry Parks, center George White, fullback Glen Jones, guard Don Randall and tackle Charles Glen would all make the All-City team. Bevil would receive a scholarship to Vanderbilt, serve in Vietnam, earn a law degree at the University of Tennessee, become an assistant district attorney and Hamilton County criminal judge. He died of cancer in 2005.

One story about Steve was that he almost got knocked out on a play on the sidelines and landed next to where Coach Farmer was standing. Stan dropped to his knees and allegedly said, "Damn it Steve, get up. We are behind!" Bevil jumped up, ran back into the game and scored a touchdown on the next play!

Bobby Etter, University of Georgia. Photo courtesy of Central High.

Charles Glen received a scholarship to Auburn University but had to receive some inspiration from Coach Farmer to obtain it. Auburn scouts had come to watch Glen in a game and he performed poorly the first half.

During the halftime break Coach Farmer administered one of his physical motivation techniques on Glen, and the player responded with an outstanding performance during the second half which resulted in Auburn offering him a scholarship. He also would have an excellent college career with the Tigers and would eventually be drafted by a National Football League team, the New York Giants. He died in 2014.

Brothers Harry and Dickie Phillips sign Grants-In-Aid to Georgia as coaches Etter and Farmer look on. Photo courtesy of Central High.

Quarterback and kicker Bobby Etter set a city-wide record for converting thirty-four extra points. He would receive a scholarship to the University of Georgia, would later play professionally for the Atlanta Falcons and would also be voted into the Central Athletic Hall of Fame in 2014 to join his father, Coach E.B. Etter and brother, Gene.

End Scott Campbell and tackle Dickie Phillips would provide the leadership for the team as captain and alternate captain. Another team honor for the 1962 squad, in addition to being undefeated and winning a State Championship, was the recognition of being ranked as the fifth best high school team in the nation.

1962 would also bring many honors to Head Coach E.B. Etter, who was recognized by both the *Chattanooga Times* and *Chattanooga News-Free Press* as "Coach of the Year." The 1962 team earned Coach Etter his seventh state championship during the twenty years he had served as Central's football leader.

Coach Etter was recognized as an innovator and was acknowledged as the "brains" of the Central dynasty. Coach Farmer was equally recognized as the motivator of the players to do their best and he was truly "adored" by them. The players respected Coach Etter. They loved Coach Farmer.

An example of how Coach Farmer stood up for his players took place in the Knox Central game in Knoxville. A big fight among the players took place and one of the opposing team's coaches grabbed one of the Central players. Katherine told one of Central's former players, John Childers, to go to the fight to keep Stan from hitting the coach. John arrived just in time and John threatened to kill the coach if he touched any Central player.

The matter eventually calmed down, and in later years Coach Farmer and the Knoxville coach would be assigned as roommates when they attended a certification school at

Peabody College in Nashville after a driver's education curriculum had been placed in the high schools of the state. The two had a good laugh about the incident and became friends while at the school.

A humorous incident occurred at the expense of Coach Les Newton when the Pounders travelled to Elizabethton in upper east Tennessee with the team's regular bus driver, Red Brown. Fearing they were getting lost and might be late for the game, Newton stuck his head out of the bus and asked a farmer riding his tractor, "Which way to Elizabethton?"

The rural farmer replied, "Why don't you ask the bus driver?"

This combination was responsible for the outstanding success of the Central football teams.

1963 Captains, Freddy Steward and Johnny Slaten. Photo courtesy of Central high.

1963 Pounder squad. Photo courtesy of Central High.

1963

With the graduation of many seniors on the state championship 1962 team, an expected decline was anticipated for 1963.

Although playing well against number one-ranked Kingsport (6-0) and major rival Bradley County (7-6) the Pounders were only able to achieve a record of five wins, five losses, and one tie. Fullback John Slaten served as captain of the 1963 squad and guard Freddie Stewart was alternate captain.

1964

As expected the 1964 squad rebounded to a fine record of nine wins, one loss, and a tie and won the county championship in Hamilton County. With only one loss to Tullahoma (14-12) and a tie with traditional foe, Kingsport (0-0) the Pounders had a fine season.

Serving as captain for the Pounders was tackle Max Smith, and halfback Steve Thompson was alternate captain.

1964 Captains, Steve Thompson and Max Smith. Photo courtesy of Central High.

Jerry H. Summers
~ 113 ~

1964 Pounder squad. Phot courtesy of Central High.

Stanly J. Farmer: We Called Him Coach
~ 114 ~

STATE 1965 CHAMPS

Central 20 Sevierville 0
Central 31 City 3
Central 33 Soddy Daisy 6
Central 13 Bradley 12
Central 34 Brainerd 0

Central 29 Red Bank 7
Central 6   Gainesville 7
Central 21 East Ridge 7
Central 14 Knox Central 7
Central 41 Notre Dame 6

MENINAK BOWL
Central 26 Englewood 6

1965 State Champs. Photo courtesy of Central High.

Max's mother used to come to watch practice every day. Coach Farmer complained that her presence required him to watch his language. One day he told Max that he had a problem because, "He couldn't even say 'crap' around the practice field anymore!"

Max looked at him seriously and said, "That's alright, Coach; she says worse."

1965

This year would mark the return of the Purple Pounders to state championship status in Tennessee as they collected the seventh title earned by Coach E.B. Etter's teams since he came to Central in 1942.

The Pounders won nine games while losing only to Gainesville, Florida. Undefeated in Tennessee, the squad remained number one in both the U.P.I. and Associated Press polls throughout the season.

Central returned to Jacksonville, Florida and successfully ended the season in the annual Meninak Bowl by defeating Englewood.

1965 Captains Phil Lewis and Steve Carroll. Photo courtesy of Central High.

Stanly J. Farmer: We Called Him Coach
~ 116 ~

1966 Pounders squad. Phtoo courtsy of Central High.

Guard and alternate captain Steve Carroll and fullback Eddie Hudson were both awarded scholarships to the University of Tennessee.

Carroll would have an outstanding career at the University of Tennessee at Knoxville and would be inducted into the Central Hall of Fame in 2016. He died the same year.

1966 Captains Buzz Adams and Denny Painter. Photo courtesy of Central High.

1966 Coaching Staff: Wayne Huling, Jake Seaton, E. B. Etter, Jack Archer, and Stanley Farmer. Photo courtesy of Central High.

**In Honor Of
Coach Stanley J. Farmer**

1966—Civic Bowl Champions

The 1966 Pounders squad had a record of 9 wins and only 2 losses and ended the season with a win in the Civic Bowl in Tullahoma. Quarterback and co-captain Denny Painter was awarded a scholarship to Vanderbilt University, and halfback Mike McCoy received a grant-in-aid to the University of Georgia. Halfback Buzz Adams and Painter served as captains for the 1966 team. Former 1960 quarterback Wayne Huling was added as an assistant coach to replace Coach Jimmy Hale.

An unexpected honor came to Coach Farmer when the 1966 Central annual, *The Champion,* was dedicated to him. The paragraph on page 17 of that year's publication is self-explanatory and clearly states the respect that Coach Farmer received from the student body:

> In appreciation of his loyalty to Central and his determination towards keeping Central "Number 1," it is with genuine pleasure that we dedicate this 1966 CHAMPION to Coach Stanley Farmer.
>
> For nineteen years Coach Farmer has demanded the best from his linemen on the football field. His inspiration to the boys year after year has been a deciding factor in the success of our football teams, with the year's team winning the seventh state championship of his career.
>
> We will always be grateful for Coach Farmer's devotion to Central High School and we wish for him many more successful years of coaching.

A pleasant side note was that the three class presidents, senior Steve Carroll '66, junior Buzz Adams '67, and sophomore Mike Perkins '68, were all football players.

Coach Farmer and class presidents Carroll, Adams and Perkins.

1967

Under the leadership of halfback and captain Mike McCoy and fullback and alternate captain Gary Hamrick, the Pounders achieved a record of 7 victories, 2 losses and 1 tie and a second place finish in the Hamilton Interscholastic League (HIL) in the AA Division Team and Captain.

Although Central won the Bradley County game 26-7 on September 29, the game resulted in a fatal injury to end Mike Perkins on the first play of the second half of the game. Whenever a player was injured, Coach Farmer would signal to Mrs. Farmer, and she would immediately take the young

1967 Captains, Mike McCoy and Gary harrick with coaching staff: Seaton, Archer, Farmer, Test and Etter. Photo courtesy of Central High.

man to Campbell's Clinic on McCallie Avenue for treatment. Dr. Earl Campbell, Sr. had been Central's team doctor for many years.

Mike Perkins had originally suffered a concussion in the Baylor game the week before the Bradley County game when he had taken a hard hit to the head.

Dr. Guy Francis was on duty and after examining Mike determined that the young man had previously sustained a broken leg that had never been properly set. Dr. Francis told Mike that he could not play football until he was seen by Dr. August McCravey, a neurosurgeon.

Mike went to see the doctor and was told to come back at the end of the week. He report-

1967 Pounder squad. Photo courtsy of Cental High.

edly did not go see Dr. McCravey the second time but told Coach Etter and Coach Farmer that he had been released to play. He played in the first half of the Bradley Central game but collapsed and died shortly into the second half.

The death of Mike Perkins had an astounding effect on both Coach and Mrs. Farmer. Mike had come from a poor family background and the Farmers were trying to get him to come live with them. He refused their offer but was at their house every weekend. Coach Etter knew of Mike's poor situation and requested Coach and Mrs. Farmer make certain that he got something to eat over the weekend.

After he collapsed on the field, Mike was taken to Erlanger Hospital. He died two days later. Coach Farmer was crushed with his death. He would often put his head on the kitchen table and sob and then blame himself for not taking Mike to the hospital. Mike's economic situation was so bad that he had seen a football scholarship as the only way to make something of his life.

Mike was laid to rest at the National Cemetery and Central paid for the entire funeral. Mike was memorialized by having his jersey number 80 retired, and to this date it is the only one that has not been worn by any player for each year.

Mike McCoy, son of another legendary Central player in the 1945-1946 season, Bob McCoy, was awarded a scholarship at the University of Georgia and would later become a physician.

The 1967 Pounders would be the first squad that would include African-America players since integration had taken

In Memoriam

". . . The cold and lifeless body
That was once a mighty king,
Now lies there in the silent hall.
It's odd what death can bring . . ."
—Marcia Gulas

THOUGH ITS JOB'S COMPLETED

Old Central's time is nearly up:
She'd go on if she could.
They'll just build on in Harrison;
That's probably twice as good.

No other school in Tennessee
Has honors that compare,
'Cause when Central is competing,
First place she will not share.

In football, or any other sport,
We use head and shoulder.
People say, "The reason you win,
'Cause ya'lls' boys are older."

One thing that's famed more than the rest,
You can always hear it.
It never fails; it's always there.
That old Central Spirit.

Many have tried to surpass us.
Their tries were very bold.
We'll cherish those fighting school colors,
Our own PURPLE and GOLD!

Though its job may be completed.
The new school on its way,
I'd rather wear a steel helmet
At old Central any day.

— Mike Perkins

Memoriam to Mike Perkins in The Champion *courtesy of Central High.*

place in the Hamilton County school system. Ben Sandefur '68, James Favors '68, and Henry Radford '70, were the first black players to wear the Purple and Gold on the gridiron.

Reuben Justice '70, would become the fourth minority player for the Pounders.

Reuben, after graduating from MTSU, became a respected educator in the Chattanooga school system. His fondest memory of Coach Farmer and Katherine is how they tried to make certain that all the players and students were treated equally, especially the African American members on the team and in school.

Reuben Justice. Photo courtesy of Central High.

1968—Cystic Fibrosis Bowl

The Pounders achieved a record of ten victories and suffered only one loss to Red Back (14-7) and finished the season ranked number six in the State. The final game was a bowl game against the Cookeville Cavaliers (34-14) in the Cystic Fibrosis Bowl.

A significant accomplishment was achieved by Coach E.B. "Red" Etter as he won his 200th victory while coaching Central on September 21, 1968. For this honor he was selected as the *Chattanooga Times* "Coach of the Year."

1968 Pounder squad. Phto courtesy of Central High.

The team was led by tackle and captain Tim Thornhill and fullback and alternate captain Rick Holder.

During the trip to winning 200 games, Coach Etter and Coach Farmer molded the character of hundreds of youth both on the sports playing fields, in the classroom, and in their personal lives. Several players earned post season honors.

1968 Captains Rick Holden and Tim Thournhll. Photo courtesy of Central High.

Halfback Reuben Justice received an Honorable Mention All-State Designation and was selected for the All-City team. He would later attend Middle Tennessee State University and establish several offensive records. He would be selected as a member of the second class of inductees in the Central Athletic Hall of Fame in 2014.

Tackle Tim Thornhill would also receive Honorable Mention All-State honors and was selected for the All-City team. Center Bobby Downs, guard David Carroll, and Mike Reno would also be selected for the All-City first team. Guard Earl Newport, and halfback Joe Gibson would be selected for the All-City second team. Finally quarterback Pat Chadd, halfback Danny Adams, fullback Rick Holder and end Ron Holder would all be Honorable Mention for the All-City squad.

Those eleven players would be recognized in some degree for their excellent performances during the 1968 season.

1969—Civic Bowl

The end of the Etter-Farmer football dynasty would come to a finale after the 1969 season as Coach Etter retired from the Hamilton County Education system and was hired as the new football and baseball coach at Baylor on the Tennessee River.

Several factors may have entered into that decision. The TSSAA had ruled that Central could not continue to play its game at the University of Chattanooga's Chamberlain Field because it provided a recruiting advantage to play football games at a college setting.

The Hamilton County Board of Education also imposed a "free recruiting" ban, prohibited players from living outside of a designated zone and going to Central.

The Purple Pounders under the recruiting personality of Coach Farmer and Coach Etter's coaching reputation had always attracted excellent athletes from East Ridge, Brainerd, Signal Mountain, Chattanooga Valley, Red Bank and other areas. Both of Coach Etter's sons, Gene and Bobby, lived with their parents and commuted to Central with their father from Red Bank.

1969 Captains Bobby Downs and Jim Barclay with Coach Red Etter. Photo courtesy of Central High.

 The Central Alumni had given Coach Etter a 1955-56 Mercury station wagon that he used in commuting back and forth to Central. It was not unusual for the vehicle to make stops in White Oak, North Chattanooga, and along Bailey Avenue to pick up Central players to take to school. The station wagon would often arrive fully loaded.

 Coach Etter's leaving Central was noted with a going away ceremony in the new Central gymnasium. He had won 7 football state championships and two baseball state championships in his 27 years at Central, and he had established the premier athletic program in the State of Tennessee. Many former players and students were disappointed with his leaving.

1969 Pounder squad. Photo courtesy of Central High.

However the added benefits that could be obtained at Baylor and the imposition of tighter regulations on the recruitment of athletes probably had a lot to do with his decision.

During the 1969 season the Pounders achieved a record of an 8 win, 3 loss season and a trip to the Civic Bowl in Tullahoma, Tennessee, against Nashville Madison.

The highest post season recognition was given to fullback Henry Radford who received Honorable Mention All-State recognition as well as being selected for the All-City First team. Henry would be offered a scholarship to the University of Miami, Florida. Guard Alan Houts and center Bobby Downs would be selected for the All-City First Team and safety Mike Cagle, tackle Mike Underhill, end John McHarge, and flanker Johnny Turner would all be chosen for the All-City second team. Captains for the year were Bobby Downs and Jim Barclay.

Although the football arena, Frawley Field, had burned down in the 1950's, the Hamilton County Board of Education had made no effort to rebuild the stadium or select another location. It was only after the Central High Alumni Association set up a special committee under the leadership of Ray Moss, Jr. that the Pounders built a new stadium with private money on Highway 58.

The facility was named War Memorial Stadium/Etter-Farmer Field honoring the soldiers from Central who gave their lives in combat. The playing surface honored esteemed football Coaches E.B. Etter and Stan Farmer.

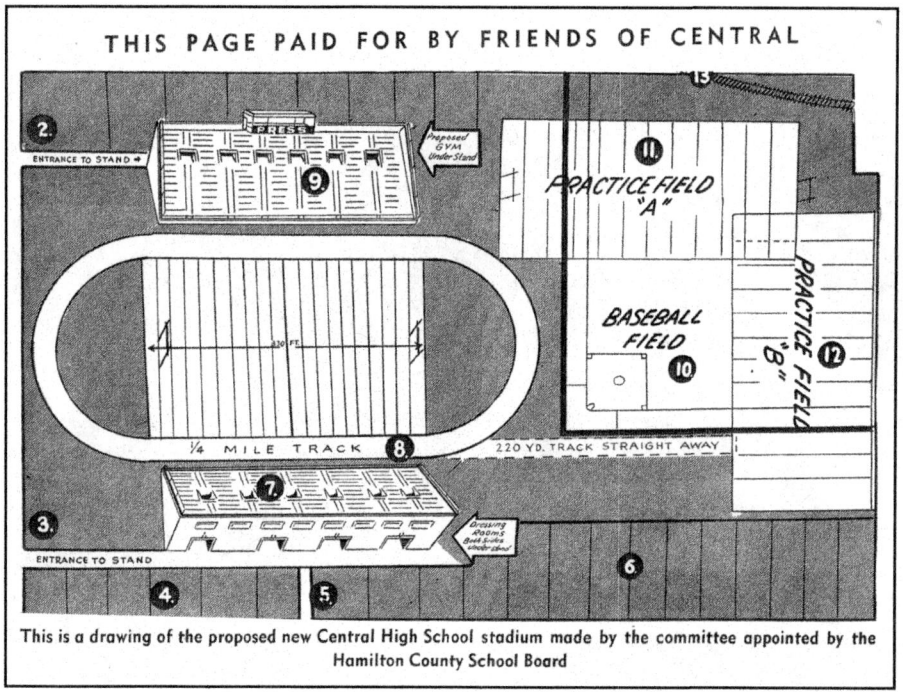

Proposed Central Sports Complex, 1963. Photo courtesy of Central High.

1970

With Coach Etter leaving to go to Baylor, Coach Farmer also decided that it was time for him to retire from coaching. He accepted the off field position of Assistant Principal to Principal Hobart Millsaps. Although he was functioning in another role, his personality and love of Central continued to endear him to all of the students at the Highway 58 school.

Principal Millsaps had been elected as President of the National Association of Secondary Schools and would be absent from Central much of the year. With the strong lead-

23 years of championship team coaching. Coach E. B. "Red" Etter and Coach Stanley J. Farmer. Photo courtesy of Central High.

ership of Stan Farmer, the school continued to function efficiently.

Although it was anticipated that Coach Jack Archer would become the head football coach when Coach Etter left, he suddenly decided to accept a similar position in the state of Georgia at the Lakeview - Fort Oglethorpe High School. Former University of Chattanooga football player Joe Lee Dunn was selected to lead the Pounders into a new era. Coach Jake Seaton and newcomer Bob Thompson had been hired to replace Coach Farmer which comprised the 1970 coaching staff.

Unfortunately the Pounders had lost many outstanding players from the previous year and fell to a one win, eight loss, and one tie. The disastrous season included a loss to longtime arch rival City High by a score of 28-6. Guard Tommy Gulas was the only Pounder to be selected to the All-City First team for the year.

Longtime Central supporter and former player, Jerry Perry, displaying some artistic talent, created a satirical collection of cartoons which memorialized Coach Farmer's method of instruction and teaching during his tenure as Central's line coach.

Cartoon courtesy of Jerry Perry.

Cartoon courtesy of Jerry Perry.

Chapter VII

Assistant Principal

Many people wondered if Coach Farmer could make the transition from coaching to being just an administrator when he accepted the position as athletic director and assistant principal upon the retirement of longtime assistant principal Everett O'Neal in June, 1970.

Mr. O'Neal had faithfully served on the Central faculty since 1943. He was a talented musician and started Central's first Swing Band. In that capacity his group performed in many school events and the group was called "Snake O'Neal and his Ragtime Band." He was sometimes referred to with that title behind his back but never to his face. He resigned for health reasons and died shortly thereafter in September leaving his wife and two children who were also Central graduates. Son, Everett W. O'Neal '56, and daughter Elma O'Neal Morris '60, were both loyal Purple Pounders.

The loyalty and talents of Mr. O'Neal helped the school transition from Dodds Avenue to Highway 58 to be smoother than expected.

With his military experience as an officer and athletic director, Farmer became a valuable ally to Principal Hobart Millsaps, who had become principal at Central in 1950. Millsaps replaced Stacy Nelson as the fourth and last principal

Archer, Farmer Officially Named To Top Athletic Posts at Central

HEAD CENTRAL ATHLETICS—The Hamilton County Board of Education today named two athletic appointments for Central High School. Pictured, from left, are Sam McConnell, superintendent, Hamilton County schools; Stan Farmer, athletic director; Hobart Millsaps, Central High principal, and Jack Archer, head football coach.—(Staff photo by John Goforth.)

By REX SANDERS
News-Free Press Staff Writer

The Hamilton County Board Education today officially named Jack Archer head football coach and Stan Farmer athletic director at Central High School.

Both appointments had been expected as they will succeed E. B. (Red) Etter, who resigned recently to become head football coach and athletic director at Baylor School.

In other action before the board, members of the Central High School Alumni Association and Central High School Boosters Club asked for matching funds to construct a football stadium at the new Harrison facility.

The group did not mention a specific amount in its request to the board. There was not an immediate estimate of a cost of a stadium.

Central High School has been without a football stadium since the late 1940s, when it ceased playing football at Frawley Field and held its games at Chamberlain Field.

Last year the University of Tennessee at Chattanooga, which operates Chamberlain Field, would not permit high school games on its field.

Announcement February 19, 1970, of appointment as Athletic Director. Soon Farmer would become Assistant Principal. Courtesy of Chattanooga News-Free Press.

at the "old" Central on Dodds Avenue. Under his leadership Central would win recognition as a national Bellamy Award School in 1963 and a National School of Excellence Award in 1987.

The departure of Etter to Baylor and Farmer going into an administration position at Central meant the "dynasty in foot-

The old Central High School was in this building on Dodds Avenue from 1907-1968. Photo courtesy of Central High.

The present school on Highway 58. The inaugural class was 1969. Photo courtesy of Central High.

ball" had come to an end. While there would be other winning teams and outstanding individual players, the Pounders would no longer be one of the most feared elevens in the Deep South.

While the demise of football excellence must have been a disappointment to Coach Farmer, it did not show in his continued support and dedication to Central.

In his new role as athletic director, he supervised all of the various athletic teams. He remained "Coach Farmer" and maintained the high standard of respect with the students that he had always had on and off the gridiron. Farmer became an effective administrator and assistant to Principal Hobart Millsaps.

He had been the heart of the Pounder football teams and he displayed the same high level of enthusiasm as a cheerleader for the school's numerous activities which further endeared him to the students and parents. While the decline in the success of the football squads must

Pounder memorabilia. Photo courtesy of Chattanooga News - Free Press.

> ### Mr. Farmer Recieves Promotion from Head of the Physical Education Department to Assistant Principal
>
> *Mr. Stanley Farmer served as head of the Physical Education Department for thirteen years. He coached linemn for twentypfour. having been appointed assistand principal this year, he was responsible for the school in the absence of Mr. Millsapy.His rapport with students and faculty enabled him to fulfill well hsi responsibilities.*

Promotion to Assistant Principal. Courtesy of Central High.

have hurt him inside, he never wavered in his support for the squads out on the field wearing the Central colors.

In 1974 Millsaps had taken a strong stand against the ruling made by the Hamilton County Board of Education that students zoned for City of Chattanooga schools could not attend Central. Although unsuccessful in his fight against the ruling, he and Coach Farmer worked together to alleviate the problems of annexation by Chattanooga in many areas where Central students found themselves residing in city zones.

Part of Coach Farmer's duties consisted of making announcements on the school intercom. Kip Henley '78, recalls the difference between his presentation and that of the school secretary, Mrs. Ellis, in her soft and beautiful voice.

Senioe Poundere cheerleader. Photo courtesy of Central High.

After wishing everyone a good morning she would turn the microphone over to Coach Farmer, and he would sound like a drill sergeant in a loud booming voice stating, "I've got these smokers going in these bathrooms, and if I catch you, you've had it!"

Ironically there was an outdoor place on the premises called "Farmer's Square" where smoking was allowed. The smoking habit he had acquired while in the Marines overseas hopping from Saipan, Trench, and Iwo Jima caused him to allow smoking in that restricted area but no marijuana.

During the 1970-1978 era Coach Farmer lost most of his hair but not his enthusiasm for Central. He and Principal Millsaps would regularly be cheerleaders at the various sporting events.

In order to adjust to the changing times he donned a wig and held a handful of flowers to let students know he was capable of bridging the generation gap in order to get through to them.

His change may have been precipitated by a dinner at Fehn's Restaurant with Coach, Katherine, their daughter, Kathy, and one of her college friends from Tennessee Tech, Kenny Bryan. Kenny would often come to Chattanooga and stay with the Farmer's family whom he stated, "treated me like a son."

Coach Farmer for some unknown reason started a rant about hippies, long hair, and headbands. Katherine unsuccessfully tried to steer the conversation to another subject. A series of kicks under the table from mother and daughter produced several grunts from Coach with no termination of

Cheerleading team assistant Prinicpal Stan Farmer, left, and Princiapal Hobart Millsaps, right. Photo courtesy of Central High.

Coach Farmer, bridging the generation gap. Photo courtesy of Central High.

his verbal attack on the hippies and their attire. Finally Coach said, "Kathy, why are you kicking me?"

Both Katherine and Kathy then told him, "Kenny has long hair and a headband."

This incident may have altered Coach's thoughts about young people with long hair and headbands that resulted in him donning the wig as assistant principal. After serving his second year in the assistant principal's office, Coach Farmer was described in the school annual as:

"Showing a helpful and courtesy manner in his encounters with students and faculty."

"Above all, his qualification for the position of assistant principal was exceeded by his cheerful attitude and ability to understand students and their problems."

A simple sign on his desk "We try to understand" assured the students that his door was always open to go in and discuss their problems.

Sign on Coach Farmer's desk. Photo courtesy of Central High.

Assistant Principal Farmer bridging the generation gap with Gary Templeton. Photo courtesy of Central High.

Chapter VIII

Central Principal
1977-1978

When Hobart Millsaps retired in 1977, assistant principal Stanley J. Farmer was the obvious choice to succeed him. His coaching experience, and seven years as assis-

The Farmer bear hug applied to class presidents, senior Greg Clark, left, and junior, Charlie Steinmetz, right. Photo courtesy of Chattanooga News-Free Press.

tant principal had made him well prepared to assume the top leadership position at Central. His cooperative relationship with Mr. Millsaps and the assumption of the principal's duties at certain times added further to his management skills.

But perhaps his greatest attribute was his uncommon ability to connect with the thousands of young men and women that he had come in contact with during his life.

Whether teaching, disciplining, or just hugging the students to let them know that he cared about them, these were part of the characteristics that allowed him to achieve success in his chosen field.

With the help of assistant principal J.D. Carnes who had transferred from Ooltewah High School, Farmer led the school's functions as an institution of learning for over 1,000 young people. Although handling more paperwork as principal, Coach Farmer stayed heavily involved in all activities of the school.

As a former football coach, he proudly assumed the role of head cheerleader for the various Purple Pounder athletic teams. He often wore one of his favorite state championship letter jackets.

As a retired military officer in the Navy assigned to the Marines Corps, he supported the ROTC regiment at Central and continued encouraging young people to be involved in the armed forces. He was proud of the fact that former Central quarterback Bobby Rudesil '55, and kicker

Jim Barclay '70, had graduated from West Point. He also shared in the honor that reflected on Central when Vance Fry

"Head cheerleader" in one of his favorite state championship letter jackets.

'54, became an admiral in the Navy as well as numerous other Central students who served their country in a branch of the services.

Although he felt honored when the football field surface had been named "Etter-Farmer Field" in the 1970's, he was especially happy that the stadium had been designated "War Memorial Stadium" in recognition of Central students who had fought and died in defense of their country.

Presentation of ROTC Sponsors. Photo courtesy of Central High.

With the Central High ROTC Color Guard. Photo courtesy of Central High.

In spite of the increased work load that he had incurred, Coach Farmer still loved to commingle with all of the students. Meeting with younger students at Hunter Middle School, he encouraged them to attend Central.

On occasion he had the opportunity to impose one of his trademark "bear hugs" as a gesture he held for the love of his students. Presiding at such enjoyable events such as pep rallies, welcoming Astronaut Alan Bean to speak to the student body, or attending any event that pertained to Central were part of his continued devotion to Central that had begun in 1947 and remained until his final days in 1996.

Visit from astronaut Alan Bean. Courtesy of Central High.

Bellamy Award presentation. Photo courtesy of Central High.

Principal Farmer with Kathy Farmer and student representative, Jack Kilgore, in Billings, Montana, for the Bellamy award presentation.

Central having won the prestigious Bellamy Award honoring Francis Bellamy, author of the Pledge of Allegiance, was entitled to have its principal and a designated student travel to the year's national awards ceremony held in Billings, Montana in 1963. It was traditional that each previous winner and the new honored school would swap gifts. Central received an Indian headdress from the winning Montana school.

Coach Farmer had received a grotesque statue from his daughter which he looked at every morning, and he said to himself, "I hope I'm not in that kind of mood today." Other Central memorabilia were located at various places in his office.

Memorabilia. Photo courtesy of News - Free Press.

For the last time he sang the *alma mater* with the seniors at graduation.

His closing remarks as he concluded his thirty-one years or service to Central were, "I've never minded one time getting out of bed to come to Central."

A retirement party was planned for the last month of Coach Farmer's tenure at Central by a committee headed by former Central students and athletes Larry Clingan, Buck Gaddis, Bob Holmes, Yvonne Newell, Assistant Principal J.D. Carnes and teacher, Jeanette Crawley.

Singing the alma mater *for the last time. Photo courtesy of Central High.*

The "arrest" of Stan and Katherine at Mock Trial. Photo courtesy of Farmer family.

Mock Trial of Stan and Katerine Farmer. Photo courtesy of Farmer family.

Prominent citizens and politicians gathered to pass judgement on Coach Farmer's record at Central accumulated over the thirty-one years. A crowd of over two hundred enjoyed a "mock trial" presided over by Hamilton County Circuit Judge

Mock Trial verdict. Photo courtesy of Farmer family.

William "Chink" Brown, '58. Judge Brown had been an All-State quarterback on the state championship football team in 1957.

Another member of that year's squad, Sergeant James "Happy" Mallett of the Chattanooga Police Department arrived with several members of "Chattanooga's finest." After hearing the various charges presented by special prosecutors Terrell Fugate, J.T. Vick and assistant district attorney Steve Bevil, '62, a quick verdict of "guilty" was rendered against Coach Farmer and Katherine. They were immediately arrested and placed in handcuffs, which briefly caused a little consternation by the two honorees. They were sentenced to receive numerous gifts in their honor and in appreciation of their service to Central.

Those in attendance waited with anticipation as their beloved teacher and ex-coach rose to speak in his loud voice which was the basis for one of his nicknames, "Boomer."

Lighter moments of the "Trial": Red Etter, Katherine, Stan, Kathy, and Jimmy Park.

Other "Trial" attendees: Ernie McCarson, Stan, Katherine, Terry Parks, Johnny Slaten, Bobby Slaton. Photo courtesy of Chattanooga Times.

It was not to be. The emotion of the time overwhelmed the ex-war hero, and it was the first time he had ever choked up despite his experience in football, Iwo Jima, Saipan and Tinian.

His prepared but unspoken thoughts were later given to Buck Johnson, *Chattanooga Times* sportswriter.

He meant to say, "The main thing in my life has been the kids. Your planning committee has done a magnificent job. It has gone beyond all expectations showing appreciation for what I've tried to do.

Listen, I'm not used to talking, I'd rather give and I'm really embarrassed to be on the receiving end.

I can't say enough about Central people. Everything I've put into this school has been returned threefold.

I accept this with great humility and will see that my hat will remain the same size."

He later met with Katherine, Kathy, and Jimmy Pack. They also were with Ernie McCarson, Terry Parks, and the Slatten brothers, Johnny and Bobby.

This ended the official connection to Central High School by Coach and Katherine. However many events would take place from this date until September 16, 1996, that would indicate that the mutual love between the Farmers and Central High School would not end.

After his death in 1996, the memories of Coach Farmer were further perpetuated in the 2009-2010 school year when "Stan the Pounder Man" was adopted as the official mascot of the school.

Katherine Farmer with mascot "Stan the Pounder Man." Photo courtesy of Central High.

Chapter IX

Retirement

After retirement, the Farmers settled down to a quieter but still active existence.

Travelling to various locations, gardening, and frequenting flea markets were all part of their routines yet maintaining contact with former Central players and students remained a high priority.

Upon running into a former student, Coach Farmer would always inquire as to what and how they were doing and their family life. Often they would reminisce about the days at Central and any particular event(s) that the two had shared together. No student ever walked away from those conversations without the feeling that Coach Farmer still cared about them.

In September 1980, Coach Farmer was honored by the Scrappy Moore Chapter of the National Football Foundation's Hall of Fame at a luncheon along with Coca Cola Executive Robert T. Davis, former Georgia Tech All-American. They were recognized for their contributions to amateur football over the years.

Arthur Hall, President of the local Chapter, in making the announcement of the award said, "He has been an inspiration to high school athletes for many, many years. What he has

1980 National Football Hall of Fame Award Presentation: Arthur Hall, Stan Farmer, Mrs. Scrappy Moore, Bob Davis, Jim Dowell. Photo courtesy of Chattanooga Times.

done for football will never be all counted. He has more friends throughout the city than most anyone who ever coached."

In later years, Central honored Coach Farmer by designating a portion of the school property as "Stan Farmer Square."

Former Central football player and later football coach on Highway 58, John Crawford '68, has a different recollection of another "Farmer's Square" at the Dodds Avenue school.

Smoking had not been completely banned from designated areas at Dodds Avenue but it was restricted to upper classmen. Crawford as a seventh grade student had become

Stan Farmer Square on Highway 58. Photo courtesy of Farmer family.

enamored by the group of guys who hung out in the alley behind the school in the "smoke hole." One day he succumbed to the temptation and bummed a cigarette from one of the older guys. He lit up and was puffing away when he heard a familiar voice from above, "Crawford ... get in here, up to the gym, now!" He had observed John's prohibited act from his gym office directly above the alley.

After informing the young man of the illegality of his act and warning him of the consequences of smoking at an early age, he administered punishment with the "Board of Education."

Evidently Coach Farmer had recognized the dangers of the habit that he had acquired while in the South Pacific during World War II and wanted to take an additional step to deter any further smoking.

John related, "When I got home that night my mother asked me, 'Have you been smoking today?' Then she said,

LIFESTYLE

Central Barbecue Honors Coaches

High school alumni gather for food, fun and fellowship

Coaches Stan Farmer, left, and Red Etter.

Old Timer Barbecue, July 1996. Courtesy of Chattanooga News-Free Press. Left: Stan Farmer and Red Etter; right: Jonny Penny, Jimmy Buun, George McCoy, Ben Milton and John Denney

'Did Coach Farmer paddle you?' When I admitted he had, she proceeded to paddle me again."

John related a second educational experience that he had received from Coach Farmer. He learned the lesson from Katherine Farmer after he had been teaching and coaching at Central several years.

Coach stated that he might be in trouble because he had gotten pretty rough on a sophomore tackle (John) that day. When the phone rang that night from John's mother, Stan got apprehensive. She told him that John's father had left them a few years earlier and that there was no male figure in their home.

She told Coach, "I don't care what you do, just make a man out of him."

Coach Farmer proceeded to do just that. John, by his own admission, was not considered a great football player, but he became a widely respected teacher and coach at Central in the same mode as Stan Farmer. To quote him in 2017, "I have deep respect, admiration, and love for Coach Farmer."

Crawford had the unique privilege of not only having Coach Farmer as his line coach but also worked for him when he became assistant principal and principal during John's first years as a teacher and football coach beginning in 1976.

John, getting out of college, had long hair and a mustache as part of the style of the times. Coach Farmer hired John and said, "When school starts in the fall, your face and hair need some cleaning up, right?" The young coach knew exactly what his mentor meant and he arrived at fall football practice clean shaven and with a shortened haircut.

As he later developed vascular problems with his legs, it became more difficult for Farmer to get around but he and Katherine continued to take trips along with a cane and then a wheel chair. He still wanted to be in the community in the hope of running into a former player or student and checking on them.

A gathering of several hundred past players, the current football team, and many friends of Coach Farmer and Coach E.B. Etter met at Chester Frost Park in July 1996, to honor all former Central coaches and hopefully stir up support for that year's football team. Coach Farmer welcomed the opportunity to talk to each of his former colleagues and coaches.

A group photo that fall with Coach Farmer and Coach Etter and some of the "old timers" suited up in Central uniforms was an effort to increase support for the football team.

Coaches Stan Farmer and Red Etter with some of their former players: Jimmy Pack and Chink Brown in front; Eddie Test, John Crawford, Bob McCoy, Jerry Summers, Ed Nobles, Stan Robbs

In February 1996, a not-so-surprise 83rd birthday party was given for Coach Farmer and a large crowd at Rib and Loin showed up to honor him once again. Among those attending was the legendary Bobby Hoppe.

When word got out that he was having serious health problems in 1996 and had been admitted to the Parkridge Medical Center, many former players publicly shared with the newspaper the impact he had made on their lives.

Coca Cola bottling executive Don Rockholt '56, and former Auburn fullback Ronnie Robbs '55, shared their views on Coach Farmer's role on their teenage years. Rockholt related how Coach Farmer whipped him with the "Board of Education" for misconduct, but every time he did he'd wrap those

85th birthday party, 1996. Photo courty of Farmer family.

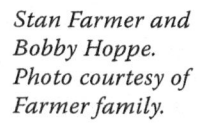

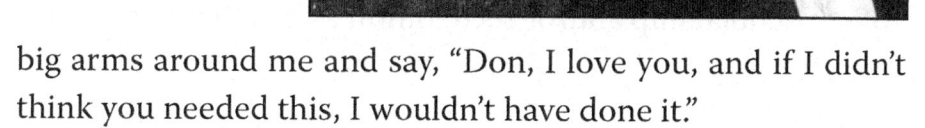

Stan Farmer and Bobby Hoppe. Photo courtesy of Farmer family.

big arms around me and say, "Don, I love you, and if I didn't think you needed this, I wouldn't have done it."

Rockholt ran into Robbie Robbs at Oscar's Restaurant on Highway 58 and the entire topic of conversation was about Coach Farmer's health.

Alan Pressley '76, an All-City player, was also the recipient of Farmer discipline but also related that after being paddled he would hug the young men. Alan said, "He knew we were good boys that just forgot how to act for a minute or two and that he was there for us if we needed him."

Roy Exum gets a bear hug. Photo courtesy of Chattanoog News - Free Press

Coach Farmer was known for demanding more from those athletes, who had the natural ability to achieve more. He rode the star players much harder than the less talented players. He pushed them to reach the maximum level of their ability and this is what often resulted in the athlete earning a college scholarship and/or recognition as an outstanding performer.

The story is repetitive from the young people that Coach Farmer coached, taught and punished at Central High.

Farmer wanted people to be as good as they could be. One day Farmer got on All State tackle Paul "Bull" Chapman and stayed on him during an entire day of practice.

The story, aged over the years as to the identity of the culprit who jokingly suggested that Bull should smack Coach Farmer, has been lost to history. The main suspects are either Bert Brown or George Shuford.

Stan with other players, clockwise from top, John Crawford, bob mcCoy, Nicki Bowman, Eddie Lance and Bobby Hoppe. Photo courtesy of Central High.

Bull's response to the suggestion has not been lost. His face scrunched up; tears filled his eyes, and he said, "I would if I didn't love him so much."

No students complained of the punishment and no parents filed a complaint with the Hamilton County School

Board. In fact if Coach Farmer had administered corporal punishment, there existed the possibility that additional punishment would be handed out at home if the parents learned of the first paddling.

Several years after his retirement and before his death, Coach Farmer asked one citizen and one lawyer if he would have gotten into trouble with school authorities or law enforcement officials for use of the "Board of Education." Both answered in the affirmative.

Chapter X

Post Central Life

In May 1978, Stan Farmer gave one of his last interviews with the media to Wirt Gammon, Jr. of the *Chattanooga Times*.

The football teams during his first two seasons at Central were mediocre, so Farmer changed his coaching style in order to get more out of his players. "I started being a clown and everything else to get the job done and make them have some pride," he said.

"They had to take it and most kids back then would take it. I wasn't mean to anybody, but I meant business. I knew most of their parents, and they didn't get riled when I shook them or gave them a good kick.

"I never kicked a boy with the point of my shoe in my life; it was always with the side of my foot. I didn't have to be mad to do it either. If a guy made tackles, he was liable to get it too. I never hurt anyone in my life. If I had, I would have quit."

Coach Etter called Farmer, "The greatest motivator I have ever seen on the football field."

Farmer was always reluctant to run down the list of the outstanding linemen that he coached, but he did acknowledge that the late Ray Moss, Jr. was one of his favorites. While

The Chattanooga Times, Sunday, May 21, 1978

On Retirement From Central

Farmer Recalls Glory Years

By WIRT GAMMON JR.

"Those who would desire to teach the young must know and understand that payment in a great part will be the love given and love received — the more given, the more received. It is my contention that in my teaching career I have been exceedingly well paid."

STANLEY J. FARMER

Stan Farmer's 31-year love relationship with Central High is coming to an end. The gruff-voiced beat of a man who turned out the tough lines which were a trademark of the Purple Pounder football teams during the glory years of the 40s, 50s and 60s is ending the official ties with the school he has served since 1947.

He turned 65 last February, but passes for a man in his early 50s. One look at his solid frame tells you he could still administer his famous breath-stopping bear hug to encourage a struggling lineman to give a little more effort on the practice field.

"I could have asked for another year and then another and probably gotten them," he says. "Maybe I could have worked four or five more years, but I've decided I'm just going to do what I want to do. I've got a boat and I'll do a lot of fishing. Katherine and I would like to do some traveling."

The way Farmer got the coaching job at Central, or better expressed, the way he almost didn't get it, says a great deal about the character of and values of the Stanley Farmer, the man.

It was right after the end of World War II and he was working as a cement salesman, traveling in Virginia and North Carolina. One day he went into the barber shop in the Masonic Building which was then across from the Krystal on Cherry Street.

"I ran into Stacey Nelson, the principal at Central," remembers Farmer. "He told me he had a coaching job open and would I be interested in it. I told him I was interested, but I had told the people I was working for I would stay with them for a year. I had given them my word and I considered it a verbal contract.

"I told Mr. Nelson if he would keep it open for a year, I would certainly consider it. Well, that was just like dropping a bone in front of a dog. Every time I was driving in that car away from Chattanooga, that job offer would come into my mind. Finally, I called Mr. Nelson and told him if he still wanted me, I would start work the next September."

The Purple Pounders did not set the woods on fire the first couple of years after Farmer arrived. Bob McCoy and Ed Nobles had led Central to a state championship in 1946, but the next two were "just so-so seasons," remembers Farmer.

"I recall that as I was starting my third season, Coach Etter remarked he wasn't looking forward to starting practice. I told him I didn't know what he was talking about. I told him, 'I don't feel that way. We've just been so-so up to now, but I'm telling you right now these kids are going to start playing football out here at Central High or there's not going to be anybody left on this field except me and you.'

Central High Coach Stan Farmer

Column by Wirt Gammon, Jr. May 21, 1978, courtesy of Chattanooga Tiemes. (Continued on following page.)

It was then, the beginning of his third year, that he changed his approach to coaching and began using the techniques which were to bear so much fruit later on, were to play a significant role in bringing football glory and championships to Central High. He wasn't emulating any coach he had ever had. If anything, he turned his real personality loose. He was doing what came naturally.

"I started being a clown and everything else to get the job done and make 'em have some pride," he says. "They had to take it and most kids back then would take it. I wasn't mean to anybody, but I meant business. I knew most of their parents and they didn't get riled when I shook 'em or gave 'em a good kick.

"I never kicked a guy with the point of my shoe in my life, it was always with the side of my foot. I didn't have to be mad to do it either. If a guy made a tackle he was liable to get it, too.

"I never hurt one in my life. If I had, I would have quit."

Red Etter has called Farmer, "The greatest motivator I have ever seen on the football field."

Football being the kind of game it is, with spirit and desire often able to overcome superior talent, a man of Stan Farmer's motivational ability was invaluable.

He had a reputation for being loud and exuberant on the practice field, but he was never abusive. He could shake a boy roughly one minute and a few minutes later hug him affectionately.

Even now he gets visits from his old players, guys who drop by to see how "Coach," is getting along.

"I think," says Farmer, "that if I've got a God-given talent, it was that I could do the things I did on the field and still keep the respect of the boys. I was able to do things with them, get things out of them, someone else may not have been able to. I think that was the successful part of my coaching.

"I wasn't the kind to stay up at night and draw plays. I knew Coach Etter would take care of that."

Even though his primary responsibility was the line, he didn't confine himself to that area. Anybody who even looked like he was loafing, to Coach Farmer not giving 120 percent was loafing, was likely to catch a blast from him.

"If a boy wasn't running with the ball the way I thought he should, and I felt some additional motivation was required, don't you think I didn't jump in and do something," he says. As he spoke, a smile broke across his face and his eyes twinkled.

Farmer politely declined to run down a list of the top linemen he has coached, saying, "I hate to discern between one or another because I didn't care whether they were the last man on the totem pole or the stars, they got a little bit of my time. I felt like I had time for them all."

He did take a moment, though, to talk about one of his favorites, Ray Moss, a tragic plane crash victim a couple of years ago.

"I really miss Ray," he began. "He was one of the best players I ever coached. A lot of Coach Farmer's psychology worked on Ray. Before we played a game at Chamberlain Field, after the captains had gone out and just before the team went out, I would walk down the line, stopping momentarily in front of the different ones I was depending on. When I'd get in front of Ray, he'd say, 'Coach, just tell 'em to play the alma mater at 8 o'clock. I'll be ready.'"

A few years ago Farmer moved from the football field to the administrative end of the school business. He swapped a coat and tie for the sweat shirt he wore so many years, but he has been no less a success in the office than he was on the football field.

The famous bear hug, so well known to his football players, is not an appropriate tack for an irritated principal to take, but he has his ways.

"Being principal doesn't operate this way," he explained, twisting his thumb hard down on his desk. "I respect these kids and then the respect comes back to me. They know when I mean business. I can't and don't try to operate from this office all together. I have to be out roaming the halls, talking to the kids, letting them talk to me."

Several years ago, Farmer resigned his coaching position and grabbed what looked like a good business opportunity. He lasted about three months. When fall football practice started, Coach Farmer was back turoring his linemen and Coach Etter was smiling again, knowing his top aide was back in the fold.

Farmer laughs about it now, calling it "my summer job." But the truth is, it simply wasn't his thing. It had no kids, no warmth.

That's the essence of Stanley Farmer, his love for kids and his warmth.

Saturday several hundred of his friends, many of them his former athletes, will get together at Central for a Stanley Farmer retirement party.

It should be a whale of a party with lots of back-slapping and story-telling. Coach Farmer will love it, not because he's the honoree, but because he'll have "his kids", around him one more time.

Wirt Gammon article continud from preceeding page.

acknowledging that he missed Ray and considered him one of his better players, Farmer related how he would stop by each player before they went out on the field to see if they were ready to play.

Moss often replied, "Coach, just tell 'em to play the *alma mater* at 8:00. I'll be ready."

In an interview with *News Free-Press* Sports Writer Dan Cook, Coach Farmer proudly recalled two Central games where the Pounders played teams led by quarterbacks who would be future All-Americans, Heisman Trophy winners and future National Football League players. Paul Hornung, the leader of the Kentucky state champions, Louisville Flaget and Central, was defending Tennessee state champs when they met in the 1950's. Hornung missed a 38 yard field goal and the teams tied 7-7.

Johnson City quarterback Steve Spurrier, who won the Heisman at the University of Florida, threw 35 incomplete passes against the Pounders as Central prevailed 14-0.

Coach Farmer also fondly recalled a trip to Memphis where the coaching staff promised the squad they would go to Elvis Presley's home, Graceland, if they won the game. They did, and the Greyhound bus drove to the rock star's home. Although the electronic steel gate was closed, one of the creative players reached around the gate and punched the electronic button which opened the gate. As the team walked up the driveway they were met by Elvis' stepfather, Vernon Presley, who warmly greeted them. He told them that Elvis had been out late and was asleep, but he would give the squad a tour of the outside of the house.

History has blurred the memories of which game, which year, and the identity of the player that opened the gate. Coach Farmer initially recalled that it was the 1954 game against Memphis Central but declined to identify the button pusher. Other players recall that it was during the 1958 season and that future Central Athletic Hall of Fame inductee George Shuford was the culprit.

Further controversy over the culprit who opened the gate at Graceland is contained in an April 19, 1992, article by Kevin Richey of the *Chattanooga News-Free Press* entitled, "Coach Stan Farmer's Eternal Football Team." Coach Farmer's recollection was that starting guard Gene McNeil "showed him how he had reached over the gate and pushed the electric button that opened the thing." Whether the act was committed by George Shuford, Bert Brown or Gene McNeil, the Purple

83rd birthday party with the boys: Dickie Phillips, Stan Robbs, Charles Preston, Larry Clingan, J. T. Vick, Jim Henley. Photo courtesy of the Chattanooga News-Free Press.

> **CHATTANOOGA NEWS-FREE PRESS—Sunday, April 19, 1992**
>
> ## Coach Stanley Farmer's Eternal Football Team
>
> **By KEVIN RICHEY**
> *News-Free Press Sports Writer*
>
> If there is or ever was such a thing as the classic American high school football coach, it is Stanley James Farmer.
>
> Immediately, an image is conjured up of a square-jawed and thick man, with a crew cut and a whistle, decked out in black high top cleats and gray sweats, and yelling at a wiry young boy trying desperately to hit a blocking dummy the right way.
>
> "You haven't got the power of a dynamo in a lightening bug's butt," the classic coach might yell.
>
> Or, he might say to his linemen before a game, "If you get your teeth knocked out, don't bring them over to the sideline to show me."
>
> But the classic coach, like a classic book or movie, is something that is valuable and endures through the years. All the yelling, sweating, wind sprints and knocked out teeth are usually forgotten and the advice and the unspoken love that were given then are what stand out even more now than the state championships.
>
> He still has the square jaw and close-cropped white hair that so many Central students over the years became familiar with, and, despite the absence of the cleats and the old sweats and whistle, one gets the feeling after spending a few minutes with the coach that he could still show a boy a thing or two about a good four-point stance.
>
> "There isn't a week that goes by that I don't talk to a few of my former players. We look out for each other, we make sure the other one is doing all right," Farmer said.
>
> "Some of them will stop by the house because they know it's as open to them as it was thirty years ago. And some of them come by the mall and have coffee with me. I'm still their coach and they know they're still my boys."
>
> As Chattanooga legendary football coach E.B. "Red" Etter's assistant from 1947 until 1969, along with assistants Les Newton and Jake Seaton, Farmer and his boys
>
> "No one around here would play us there for awhile," laughed Farmer. "We went to Miami, Atlanta, Memphis, Little Rock, Louisville, all over the place to play, and we won a lot more than we lost against those out-of-town schools.
>
> "We also played our home games at Chamberlain Field and we used to pack it," he continued. "It was some time."
>
> In the 22 years Etter and Farmer were at Central, the Pounders won an astonishing 73 percent of their games. Out of 246 played, Central won 180 and tied 12.
>
> "Coach Etter was the creative football genius," said Hamilton County Criminal Court Judge Steve Bevil, a member of the 1962 team that went undefeated and won the state championship.
>
> "He truly had a great football mind. But Coach Farmer was the man in the trenches. He was close to all the players and really was like a father figure for a lot of those guys."
>
> "I didn't think there was any way we'd beat that team," Farmer continued, "But we did, 7-0. And the next morning after the game, Chink came up at breakfast and reminded me of the deal. So, we took the bus over there and I told Coach Etter not to worry because there wasn't any way those boys were going to get inside that big gate there.
>
> "The boys were standing in front of the gate gawking at the house and all the sudden, the gate swung open and there go fifty boys sprinting up the driveway toward the front of the house.
>
> "They got up there and Chink rang the door bell and Elvis' mom and dad came to the door," Farmer continued. "His parents said Elvis was asleep, but Mr. Presley said he would show the team around the grounds since they had just put a whipping on Elvis' rival high school the night before.
>
> "When those boys got through looking around," continued Farmer, "One of my guards, Gene McNeil, showed me how he had reached over the gate and pushed the electric button that had opened the thing. And the whole time us coaches were thinking that someone up in the house had let those boys in."
>
> Stanley Farmer's football sense and ability to lead men was well honed by the time he entered the ranks as a Central coach in the fall of 1947.
>
> As a tenth grader, Farmer was denied a uniform at Central on the basis that he was too small. So, he abruptly traveled across town to City High School where in 1930, as a 125-pound center and linebacker, he made second team All-City.
>
> The next two years Farmer grew to be captain of the All-City squad, and he was named to the prestigious All-Southern team the fall of his senior year, 1932.
>
> "My college decisions came down to Loyola of the South in New Orleans and Emory and Henry in Virginia," explained Farmer. "Both schools had offered me a scholarship and without football, during those Depression times, I wouldn't have gotten to go to college.
>
> "My father took me down to the terminal station where the Choo Choo is now," continued Farmer. "In five minutes both the train going south toward Loyola was coming through and the train going north toward Emory and Henry was coming through and I still didn't know where I was going to school."
>
> As the trains approached the platform, Farmer asked his father who had purchased the boy's ticket, where he was going to school.
>
> "Son," he said to me," Farmer recalled. "I've given this some thought and I think you can get along with people of all religious persuasions however, down at that Catholic school in New Orleans, if any thing goes wrong, they'll probably cut you off before they would a Catholic boy. So, you're going on the northbound train."
>
> After graduating from college in 1937 with a degree in history, Farmer came home and taught and coached at City, spending his summers in New York City working on his masters degree at Columbia University.
>
> In the summer of 1941, Farmer joined the Navy and became a Chief Petty Officer. After a stint as a commanding officer of an oil tanker that ran oil across the North Atlantic to England, Farmer served in the South Pacific.
>
> Following combat duty at both Saipan and Tinian, Farmer landed on Iwo Jima as a Lieutenant Commander in charge of gunnery for the 26th Regiment of the 5th Marine Division.
>
> He was decorated on Iwo for bravery in the line of fire and later became a Commander in the Naval
>
> **LT. CMDR. FARMER**
> *In Jeep On Hawaii*
>
> Reserves, retiring from that post in 1970 after 23 years of service.
>
> "I treated those boys in my regiment just like I treated my football players," said Farmer. "Fair and square and tough."
>
> At his retirement party from Central in 1978, Coach Farmer summed up his 31 years as a teacher, coach, administrator, confidante, disciplinarian, friend, and father figure to scores of Central football players: "Those who would desire to teach the young must know and understand that payment in a great part will be the love given and love received — the more given, the more received. It is my contention that in my teaching career I have been exceedingly well paid."
>
> That night, Coach Farmer's boys gave he and Kathryn a month-long paid trip to Europe, but that wasn't a pay off of any sorts. Every day, week, and year the old Central boys call up their old coach or drop by the mall to have coffee and check on him.
>
> "We watch out for each other," Coach Farmer said. "That team spirit never goes away."
>
> **RED ETTER, JAKE SEATON, LES NEWTON, AND STANLEY FARMER**
> *Central High School Football Coaching Staff Pictured In 1948*
>
> Stanley Farmer was and still is a good coach, the type that was more than capable of all the stuff above. A classic through and through.
>
> Gone are the swift kicks to the rear. Still left here are the memories of things — meals, a place to stay, a new shirt or pair of shoes, a pat on the shoulder after a good game — given to boys in need.
>
> "I love those kids," said Farmer of the boys he coached, many of whom are now grandfathers. "I treated them all tough but I treated them all fair."
>
> These days, Coach Farmer can be found several times a week hanging out in the Oasis food court at Hamilton Place Mall. He sits there and talks and drinks coffee while his wife, Kathryn, gets her
>
> helped to make Chattanooga Central High School synonymous with high school football all over the south.
>
> Between 1950 and 1965, the Pounders won six state championships (four in the 1950s), had more than a handful of players named to the high school All-America team, and, for the most part dominated area and regional gridiron action.
>
> In fact, during the 1950s, not too many area teams would play the Purple Pounders in football. Between the six football seasons spanning from the fall of 1955 through the fall of 1960, Central only played area schools eight times. Bradley, which was really not an area team then, lined up and played Central every one of those years. Baylor did once and Red Bank did once.
>
> "He knew how to motivate people," recalled Harry Phillips, the quarterback of the 1962 squad and one of six players who named sons after Farmer. "I've seen him drive people to tears in practice, but he knew what he was doing. He made them a better player and a better person by pushing them."
>
> Farmer also played two home games for the serious Central athletes, who, by the way, were not allowed to eat sweets or drink soft drinks during the season. The day before games the players could not talk to girls.
>
> The week before the Memphis Central game in 1957, Chink Brown, our quarterback, who is now a Circuit Court Judge, came to me and said, 'Coach, if we beat Memphis Central, can we go see Elvis' house?'" Farmer laughed.

Courtesy of Chattanooga News-Free Press.

Pounders enjoyed their tour of the outside of Elvis' estate by his step-father.

    On his eighty third birthday Coach Farmer was honored at a dinner by several of his former players and students. As always he thoroughly enjoyed the opportunity to reminisce about the past and asked how each was doing after graduation from Central.

Chapter XI

Recollections of Former Students and Players

If everyone had responded to the multiple requests over the last few years through the "Central Connection" website and other forums for Coach Farmer remembrances, the length of this publication would be never ending.

I have chosen selectively some of the most informative responses in an effort to contribute to the unique qualities of Coach Farmer which caused him to be loved and adored by so many.

Tom Morgan '49, was a center and linebacker on the Pounder squad. He lived in St. Elmo and remembers riding to Central with Coach Farmer in his Ford Woody station wagon. Stan's wife, Katherine, would be dropped off at work and they would pick up other Central students along the route to Dodds Avenue.

Tom spoke fondly of Coach Farmer and described himself as the slowest lineman at 155 pounds on the team. He did relate that their punter in 1949, Jody Neal, was a barefoot kicker and was close to Bobby Hoppe, as they both lived in North Chattanooga.

Ted Gilreath '54, was a halfback on the Pounder squad and was also a close friend of highly sought after football prospect, Hoppe. Rumors exist that Auburn recruiters urged Gilreath to encourage Hoppe to sign with the Tigers. Hoppe reciprocated by helping Ted become a manager for the Tigers at the Plains. Gilreath's career highlight as a Purple Pounder consisted of throwing a twenty-five yard touchdown pass against Red Bank.

Henry Jones was an All City guard in 1949 but had trouble remembering the plays, and Coach Etter remarked to Henry, "Every time you think, we lose six points."

Terrell Dye and Grady Wade were valuable performers on both the 1957 state championship and 1958 state runner-up football teams. Both recall fond memories of Coach Farmer. Terrell recalls that in 1956 Coach Farmer went around to the junior high schools recruiting football players for Central. He thought that three of the players at East Lake Junior High, including Dye, were talented enough to play for the Pounders.

He drove them around the Central campus on Dodds Avenue and the new practice field in Glenwood in 1956. He talked about the football team and school for about an hour. Terrell relates that the players felt they were moving into the big time by being recruited in junior high school.

Dye, who was an honor student at Central and graduated with a degree in chemistry from Vanderbilt, asked Coach Farmer if Central offered a first year calculus course. Coach Farmer replied "Yes, I think we have some Catholics."

Dye recalls Coach Farmer coming to the Tennessee - Vanderbilt football game in 1960 with Coach Etter. The contest would be Gene Etter's last college game for UT. Dye was a sophomore who played defensive halfback for the Commodores. Grady Wade was the kickoff specialist for Vandy during his career.

In 1958 one of the players played the "water on the door" trick in the coaches locker room by placing a bucket of water above the door so it would fall when the door was opened. Water got on Coach Farmer's coat and Coach Etter was livid. He ordered Dye to lead the team in running one hundred laps before practice as punishment. After about seven laps, Dye jokingly told Coach Etter they had done ninety seven, and Etter told them to do one more lap and they would start practice.

Grady Wade '59, was also recruited by Coach Farmer to go to Central while a ninth grader at Northside Junior High School along with George Shuford, Mike O'Brien, and Buddy Norton.

In his initial conversation with Coach Farmer, Grady informed him that the City High coach had implied that he would be guaranteed a uniform and that he would "get to dress" for the games. The Maroons coach further stated that there were so many good players at Central that there was a likely chance he would not get a uniform as a sophomore at Central. Wade said that Coach Farmer went "berserk."

He said, "I'll tell you one damn thing Wade. ...If you get a uniform at Central High School it will be because you have earned it. We don't promise anyone a uniform."

Grady said that from that moment, "I was hooked to be a Purple Pounder."

He also recalled some of the more famous Farmer quotes which he used on various players:

1. "You guys look like two love birds flying backwards trying to bump butts."

2. "You couldn't p _ _ _ a hole in the snow."

3. "If I didn't love you and think you could play, I wouldn't get after you!" (He never got on any player of limited ability but who was trying.)

4. "I'm going to hit you with a blivet." (A blivet was 10 pounds of s _ _ _ in a 5 pound bag.)

Bill Freeman was a big player with a lot of potential as both a tackle and fullback, but he was basically lazy. Farmer stayed on him constantly, "Freeman, your daddy told me that if you didn't start hitting people to just kick the s _ _ _ out of you!"

As soon as Farmer said the words, Coach Newton affectionately known as "Farmer's Echo," would repeat the saying verbatim, "That's right Freeman. Your daddy told Coach Farmer that if you didn't start hitting people, he should just kick the s _ _ _ out of you."

Several years after he retired from coaching, Coach Farmer said, "Wade, if they had today's rules back then, they would have locked me up for the things I said and did, wouldn't they?"

Grady, whose father was a Chattanooga Police Department detective, agreed. The same question was put to the author several times as a practicing attorney and former prosecutor. Coach Farmer upon receiving the same affirmative answer as Grady Wade got, would always laugh.

Donnie Strickland, '60, gave a humorous non-football story about Coach Farmer. Coach Farmer would umpire baseball games in the summer and Donnie played for a team from East Ridge sponsored by Central varsity player Ken Hudgens' dad, Ray. They played under the name of Pops Drive-In. Ray was also the Coach for the team.

Coach Farmer when umpiring would not call a pitch a strike. He would always use the term "right in the skillet." He was the only umpire that deviated from the normal ball or strike calls.

George Brown ("Butch') Harless, III, came to Central as a sophomore after being asked to leave McCallie School, Rossville High School, and attending Sewanee Military Academy for only one day. When the rebellious young teenager started playing hooky at Central, he was brought before Coach Farmer. In a non-gentle gesture Coach slammed Butch against the wall and in no-uncertain terms proceeded to inform the young man of the physical consequences if he continued to skip class and misbehave. Butch has candidly admitted for the first time he was truly scared and that Coach Farmer had gotten his attention. He would be an outstanding football player and graduated in 1959.

Jerry Shuford, '61, was a three sport letterman and went to Vanderbilt University on a football scholarship. One of his major accomplishments at Vandy was against Tennessee in 1964 when he engaged in a punting duel with the Volunteers' Ron Widby, and the Commodores won 7-0.

Jerry wrote an emotional letter to the Editor in 1996 upon Coach Farmer's passing. "Coach Farmer was the richest man I have ever known. That is if you measure riches in love everyone felt for him. Coach Farmer was also the most intelligent man I have ever known. That is if you measure intelligence accumulated throughout years of hard work and association with a lot of impressable [sic] young men. And I know God's football team is better today than they were last week because, while we lost a friend, they gained a new coach."

Jim Barclay, '70, was a lineman and place kicker. Jim recalled four specific events with Coach Farmer. He observed the profound effect that the unfortunate accident and subsequent death of end Mike Perkins in the 1967 Bradley Central game had on Coach Farmer. On Saturday after the Friday night when Mike collapsed, Jim talked to Coach Farmer at the hospital and the love and emotion in his voice showed how much he cared about Mike as if Mike was his own son.

Jim Barkley and Coach Farmer at Meninak Bowl, 1970. Courtesy of Farmer family.

A second memory dealt with how much Farmer cared about his players. At a junior varsity game that Central lost, the fans for the other team began to mock and criticize the Central players. Although he was at the game only as a spectator, Coach Farmer got so mad, he was going after the accuser, but he was held back by Central players and fans. To Jim that demonstrated that Coach Farmer would really stand up for his players and that, although he might get on them himself, he wasn't going to let anyone else criticize his players because he would defend them to the end.

Medal of Honor winner Coolidge presents Army Legion of Valor Bronze Cross to Jim Barclay. Photo courtesy of Chattanooga Times.

Barclay was a place kicker but had been injured with a foot injury and could not kick field goals or extra points most of the season. However in the Meninak Bowl game at Jacksonville, Florida, in the final game of the season, he attempted and missed the extra point and Central lost 7-6. The next Monday when the players reported to turn in their equipment, Coach Farmer was there to encourage Jim to keep his chin up. Those words would be very important to the player when he played college football at Army.

In November 1969, at the official dedication of the new Central High on Highway 58 in Harrison, Jim was presented the Army's Legion of Valor Bronze Cross for achievement and outstanding academics. A lieutenant cadet colonel in the Central ROTC unit, he was presented the award by Charles H. Coolidge who was awarded the Congressional Medal of Honor for bravery in World War II. The award was one of three issued annually by the United States Army.

During his sophomore year Barclay kicked three field goals against Georgia Tech in Atlanta and the Cadets won 16-13. The next week he received a letter from Coach Farmer, who expressed how proud he was of him and said Jim, "Needed to be able to wear the same helmet size at the next week's game." Coach Farmer's words were a very timely reminder of the need for humility.

Mike Randolph '65, related a story about how Coach Farmer could be understanding in a common sense way. Mike had been out of Central for about two years. One day he was driving through his neighborhood and saw a young man who was a starter on the Pounder squad but was walking down the street when he should have been at football practice. When Mike stopped to inquire as to why he was not at the practice site, he indicated that he had quit because Coach Etter had assigned him the number 69 for his jersey. Mike took the player to Coach Farmer's home that evening, explained the situation, and the next day he returned to the squad with a new number on his game jersey.

Jimmy Cheek '58, alternate captain on the 1957 State Championship team, was president of Tennessee Wesleyan College and described Coach Farmer as follows: "It is not possible for me to remember the many lessons Coach Farmer taught me and others. However I am sure that my life and that of hundreds more has been better because of him. We loved him as he did us. He is missed but he left us with great memories and with pride that we had a chance to know him. In addition to making us better players, he made us better people."

Tommy Youngblood, '71, was a Purple Pounder for six years but became one for life when Coach Farmer asked him before his father, "Would you like to be a Pounder?"

During his junior year Tommy's mother was expecting a child, and he was summoned to the principal's office by way of the intercom. He was in Coach Farmer's Drivers Ed class and Stan asked Tommy what he had done because a student usually had gotten into trouble when summoned to the principal's office. Coach Farmer took him to the office, and when he found out his mother was about to deliver a baby, he looked at Tommy and said, "Drivers Ed trip – let's go!"

When they got back to class, Coach Farmer said, "Anyone that wants to can drive Youngblood to the hospital."

Tommy's best friend yelled out "Oh God, Coach, did you beat his butt that bad?'

When they got to the hospital, a nurse stopped them and inquired, "Sir, is that your wife?

Coach said, "If she needs to be in order for me to get this boy up there, then she is."

After the baby was delivered Coach Farmer, in the waiting room, said, "Let's go see this brother of yours."

"That day cemented in my life that Coach Stanley J. Farmer was part of my family, and that he thought of me as one of his boys."

Ray Henry, '71, expressed his opinion of Coach. "I remember like yesterday. He was a huge influence in my life and many other young men at Central. He was a John Wayne, General George Patton and Vince Lombardi all wrapped up into one. His pregame and halftime speeches were legendary. He turned many young boys into real men when they graduated from Central. One of his favorite quotes was, 'Winners never quit; quitters never win,. I never will forget the man, Coach Stan Farmer!"

Debbie Hunt Gilliland, '73, gave a female perspective of Coach Farmer's punishment style. She stated that she and three other students decided to skip class and take a fast ride in Mike Allen's Pontiac GTO. As they pulled back into the parking lot, Coach Farmer was waiting for them.

He says, "Boys, three licks. Debbie I'm calling your daddy."

She replied, "Wait, I'll take three licks; don't call," as she grabbed her ankles and took the paddling. That was the last time she skipped class. She found out later that Coach Farmer had already called her parents. Her parents trusted and respected Coach Farmer and waited until Debbie graduated before they told her that they had been called.

Another member of the Class of 1973, Cathy Barnes, remembers Coach Farmer as someone who was always encouraging the students to do better.

Douglas Gilmore, '74, was a juvenile delinquent who Coach Farmer converted into an Army Veteran, husband of 36 years, and a father of three successful children. Doug graduated from Georgia Tech with a degree in Civil Engineering.

He credits Coach Farmer with changing his life to allow him to accomplish all of the above.

Doug related how in his teens he regularly skipped school, bought beer illegally, got in fights and on one occasion stole hub caps. Principal Hobart Millsaps wanted Doug kicked out of school. The boys were caught and two sheriff's deputies were called. They interviewed them and their technique was not one good cop and one bad cop. It was bad cop, worse cop.

Coach Farmer walked into the room and asked the officers if he could speak to Doug. Coach Farmer and Doug were no strangers and Doug had met the "Board of Education" on several occasions. Farmer's paddle and Doug's backside were well acquainted.

Doug said, "Coach Farmer didn't have to move his paddle more than twelve inches and he could lift you off the ground."

As they faced each other, Coach Farmer told the young man, "Son you have a choice. You can continue to be a punk and you can ruin your life. Or you can choose to be a man. That's your choice. No one else can make it for you. If you want to be a man, I can help you. If you want to be a punk, I'll call the deputies back in."

"I told him I wanted to be a man. He told me he'd help me and he did." After having to apologize to several people, Doug grew up with the help of Coach Farmer and a few more sessions with his "Board of Education."

Coach Farmer would lecture Doug about hanging out with the right people: "Birds of a feather flock together; it's easier for a bad person to pull you down than for you to lift a bad person up; life isn't fair and life isn't easy, so suck it up and drive onward."

Gilmore credited Coach Farmer and a military sergeant with saving his life. The main thing he remembered about Coach Farmer is that he absolutely loved the students at Central High. He wanted and demanded that they succeed in life. When someone failed it bothered him. "Those he saved can never repay him." He remembered Coach Farmer with a big smile when he saw one of his boys walking in the halls of Central. He stated, "I was one of his boys."

There are hundreds, if not thousands, of stories that could be written about Coach Stan Farmer and his interactions with the students and athletes at Central High School over the 43 years. Many are serious, some funny and some sad.

Yet during the research of this book on his life, no one objected to the punishment he administered, but all cherished the thought that he cared enough about the students to want them all to succeed in life. Some would have to admit that Coach Farmer may have been the first to show a real interest in them.

No parents ever filed a complaint against Coach Farmer for the punishment he administered to their children. They knew that if he imposed it, it was justified and needed.

Coach Farmers influence reached beyond the athletes and students at Central High.

Jerry Weaver had a daughter who attended Ooltewah Middle School and was planning to go on a trip chaperoned by Kathy Farmer (Ratz) in 1994 to Hawaii, Australia, and New

Zealand. He met Stan and Katherine and was immediately impressed by their strong feelings toward young people.

In a statement styled "The Boy I Never Coached," Jerry puts in words a fitting tribute about Coach and Katherine that presents a proper summary of the qualities they possessed and the way they used these qualities to better the lives of all they touched.

> In the fall of 1993, I was given the opportunity to meet a family that I had heard so much about. My daughter was attending Ooltewah Middle School and came home and asked if it was ok for her to go on a school trip in the spring of 1994. I being a little inquisitive about the trip before knowing where the trip was to be going said yes. In a few weeks she said we had to go over to a teacher's house, and I was introduced to a school trip that involved my little daughter going to Hawaii, Australia and New Zealand.
>
> Sitting around the room was a couple that was introduced to me as Coach Farmer and his lovely wife Katherine. It was easy to see from the way that they enjoyed being around children and adults that I was going to be in for more than a trip with my daughter, but a wonderful life experience learning many wonderful stories about their journey through life. I have never been so impressed hearing about their lives and the way that Coach and Katherine affected so many people.
>
> Once my daughter and I got back from our wonderful trip with their daughter Kathy, I was exposed to the most gracious and giving couple I have ever had the opportunity to meet. The next time Coach saw me was when Katherine brought me home from the hospital to take care of me after some surgery. All Coach said when she brought me into their den was, "Can we make him comfortable, and what can I do to help?"
>
> As my stay at their house went on for a few days, I grew closer to a man that was more of a father to me than the

man who was my father. All Coach wanted to do was make me feel comfortable, wanted, and loved. He always seemed interested in what I was doing in my life with my career, my children, and my own life.

As the years began to go by, so did my knowing that I had found someone that was real and genuine. I have found that it is impossible to give back as much love and concern as I received from Coach and Katherine. My Sundays with them sitting on the screened in back porch listening to many years of wisdom and thought about family values, world affairs, local politics, other current events, sports. Leaning about the lives that they had touched over the years and how good the people had turned out. The way that certain events in people's lives were changed forever because of the positive influence from Coach and Katherine.

Even though I has such a short time with Coach, I can never forget his sayings and the way he went about enjoying life. The only man that could scold you and love you at the same time. He was more than an inspiration to his players that won so many championships. Coach gave each of his "boys" such attention that they would feel like they were the only person in his life. What a quality to be able not only coach so many, but guide their lives in such a way that he had to stand back and be proud of each and every one of his players at Central.

The hardest lesson that I leaned from Coach that was hard for me was to always look for something positive that would make someone else feel wanted and loved. Even when Coach became sick and his health began to decline, he was not bitter at God or his circumstances that would have caused others to run and hide. His cup was never half empty, but always half full or better. Coach would make all who talked to him feel like they were leading the conversation, but somehow he knew exactly how to keep people discussing the conversation in the direction he thought it should go. Assisting you in making life decision that would affect the lives of so many.

Traveling with me to take my daughter back to Tullahoma on Sundays was something he and Katherine decided that I would need some company coming back to Chattanooga. They would lean their heads out the car window so they could direct me in such dense fog that one could not see the end of the hood on the car. Eating at the restaurant at the top of Monteagle. Just enjoying life as it had been dealt him.

When it came time for him to have to spend more time in the hospital, Katherine would stay by his side at night, and I would come to relieve her around 5:30 AM each morning so she could go home, shower and get a little rest. Coach and I would sit, and I would read the paper to him. He would make comments about the different stories in the paper and would tell interesting things about the different people that he knew. Always proud of the boys that he and Katherine had recruited to play football for Central and then help them be afforded the opportunity to further their education through scholarships earned through their hard work on the football field.

Even the medical people at the hospital knew of Coach and his achievements at Central High School. I considered it an honor to have been so close to him, even though he introduced me to some of his boys that played for him as "the boy I never coached." He got some funny looks from people when he said that, but I do know that even though I only knew him for a short time before he died, he was the very best male influence that anyone could have in their lives. For all the boys that he influenced, he should have been given lifetime achievement awards. I do know that he was proud that he had gotten to be around so may boys that became such successful men as they began to grow up.

My life was changed because of Coach and Katherine. You could not order or hand pick better people to influence so many lives as did Coach and Katherine Farmer. It makes me feel so good to know that Coach has a scholarship given in his name to a deserving senior at Central High School each year. Even though he is no longer gracing us with his presence, he continues to influence and change lives of young kids that can only hear stories about the finest coach that ever coached so many boys who later became men that influence so many people in the community. So many times we forget how we got where we are today. His leadership qualities have been passed on to the many boys that he coached on the football field while showing them that making a difference in the lives that we come in contact with. Coach and Katherine have a full life giving, helping, and sharing life's experiences with so many people that they came in contact with.

Jerry Weaver

The 2017 winner of the Coach Stanley J. Farmer Scholarship to assist them in obtaining a college education was Tatum Morgan. In the essay submitted in her application for the scholarship, she vividly describes the impact that Coach Farmer had on students and athletes at both Dodds Avenue and Highway 58. The contents of the essay are a proper testimonial as to the permanent effect on students by Coach Farmer. An excerpt of the three page document in below:

"Coach Farmer is easily the most recognized name when it comes to Central High sports. … I cannot help but notice what an impact Coach Farmer made on not only the football program, but the school too. Although he is known for being such a great coach, the thing that stands out most to me is how he built traditions that are still practiced today. Coach Farmer was a passionate man who believed in hard work and having pride in being a Central High School Pounder. He also thought of Central as his family, which highly relates to me. ... Because of Coach Farmer emphasizing the tradition of hard work, it has impacted me to always put 110 % effort in whatever comes my way. ... If I leave an impact half as much as he did, I know I will be successful in life. ..."

E6   *CHATTANOOGA FREE PRESS*

Scholarship Fund Honoring Farmer

By ROY EXUM
Free Press Executive Sports Editor

A scholarship fund in memory of beloved Central High School coach Stan Farmer has been established by the school's Alumni/Supporters Association, and already over $5,000 has been raised to send deserving students to college.

The fund, which is the brainchild of avid Central supporter Jerry Summers, will be given each year to a Central High student who earns a varsity letter in athletics, who has a legitimate financial need and who meets other criteria established by a committee.

Included on the committee will be Katherine Phillips Farmer and Kathy Farmer Ratz, Coach Farmer's wife and daughter; the school principal; the school athletic director; the guidance department counselor, and Mr. Summers.

"We feel that Coach Farmer would do anything he could for a child and this only reflects the way he lived his life," said Summers. "We have had tremendous response already but feel like we've just touched the tip of the iceberg."

Serving as "decade chairmen" for the scholarship fund are Bob McCoy, '47; J.T. Vick, '49; Tommy Cox, '55; George Shuford, '59; Butch Harless, '59; Dickie Phillips, '63; Mike Randolph, '65; Ron Childress, '66; Dr. Robin Smith, '75, and Alan Presley, '76.

Those wishing to contribute to the fund may do so by mailing a check or money order to Coach Stan Farmer Scholarship Fund, c/o Central High School Alumni/Supporters Association, Central High School, 5728 Highway 58, Harrison, TN 37341.

Those desiring further information can contact Summers at 265-2385.

Chapter XII

Sportswriters Reviews

Through his career at Central beginning in 1947, Coach Farmer had remained subservient to the legendary head football coach E.B. "Red" Etter. Etter was the football "genius," Farmer was the football "motivator." To put it another way, Etter was the "brains," Farmer was the "heart." Etter could tell the boys "how to win," Farmer would make them "want to win." Together they made the Purple Pounders a winning team through Tennessee and the South for twenty-three years.

The sports editors and writers for the *Chattanooga Times* and *Chattanooga News-Free Press* held Coach Farmer in high esteem throughout his coaching and teaching career.

Two periods in Coach Farmer's life produced well written columns by a variety of writers for both papers. The first period was his announced retirement from Central after coaching, teaching, and service as assistant principal and principal in 1978. The second was the reporting of his declining health and ultimate death in 1996.

Steve Parker of the *Chattanooga News-Free Press* interviewed Coach Farmer in March 1978, about his pending retirement in an article titled, "Coach Farmer Recalls 31 Years of Loving Central." The article is reproduced on pages 196-197.

It was followed by *Chattanooga Times* sportswriter Buck Johnson in a late May article styled "Time Had Come to Say Thanks Coach Farmer."

Buck covered the retirement party held at Central that included many dignitaries, former players and coaches, all who had shared many experiences with the gentle giant that they all loved and respected.

Time Had Come to Say, 'Thanks, Coach Farmer'

Buck Johnson

It was his last hurrah.

The Saturday sounds of it reverberated through the hills of Harrison and the lure of it brought former players and students and coaches and friends from across the country to the campus of Central High School to salute "their man" and taste again the Purple and Gold pride that engulfs the Central clan.

It was Stan Farmer's day. Stan Farmer, coach, teacher, administrator, friend. It was a day, not for handshakes, but for hugging the boys of winters past. None were the physical specimens he once knew and all envied the tough, young and proud Pounders who braved the hot Saturday sun in playing the Purple and Gold football game.

These were Farmer's boys, some now with the paunches, the bald spots on their head, the stogies dangling from their lips. These were his boys, those whom he had sought; those who had athletic talent that was developed under his care. These were the heroes past, heroes Stan Farmer and Red Etter and Jake Seaton and Les Newton had shared with the community.

The ghosts of old Central dominated the new on this day because it quickly became evident that though the body was at Harrison, the heart, somehow, was still on Dodds Avenue, Glory Street, the Avenue of Champions, the Highway of Thrills that Stan Farmer helped build.

These were the men who, as boys, had shared the triumphs and tragedies of Central. They were here to salute the man who had made them want to play, to be enthusiastic and loyal to a cause. This was his gift to them.

The time had come to at least say "Thanks, Coach."

Stan Farmer's enthusiasm was then, and is now, contagious. As a coach it was a deep enthusiasm for the contest at hand and he approached each with irrepressible zest. It was this enthusiasm and knowledge of handling boys that helped Central to dominate the high school scene in a manner that may never be equalled.

Jake Seaton was the first of the other members of Etter's Fearsome Foursome to arrive. He had quickly checked his garden and headed for Harrison and a hug from Farmer. Newton and Etter would arrive later. All would be there for the big bash Larry Clingan and his steering committee had planned for the evening — the party in front of the school around the Pounder Anvil and the dinner outside between the buildings.

Visitors checked the huge bulletin boards on the press box wall where clippings and pictures of past and present Central, with the focus on Farmer, flooded memories into the minds of the older generation. The young were more interested in the football squad game and the Coke stand. The band played constantly and Pounder balloons were waved from the gathering in the stands.

"If you had done this like I wanted to, you wouldn't be going through all of this," said Catherine Farmer to her husband. She had suggested that Stan bow out quietly, an idea vetoed by her husband at the urging of his boys. "It would have been easier on us emotionally," said Mrs. Farmer, "but isn't it great to see all of these boys here today?" She and daughter Cathy, a teacher at Anna B. Lacey School, have been teasingly calling Stan the "Great Swami" in recent days.

It would be a tough day emotionally for Farmer, one that would be etched on his mind forever, but he's seen tough days before. Few are aware that this courtly and well-mannered professor has an enviable war record and is a retired Naval Commander.

Football must have been mild to his Navy man who, while being detached to the Fifth Marine Division saw action at Saipan and Tinian and was in the second wave to hit the bloody beaches of Iwo Jima. It was his division that planted the flag on Iwo Jima and an Indian friend, Ira Hayes, would be immortalized in the famous flag-raising picture from that Pacific hell-hole.

He was tough, but a softy at heart. He could flex his muscles or cry, depending on what it took to get his message across to the boys. "I'll tell you what kind of a guy he is," a former player said. "He could whip hell out of you with a paddle and you would go away feeling he had done you a favor."

A classic example of adoration.

It was a time for such stories. One making the rounds concerned the fleet Bobby Hoppe who had been reported smoking before a game in Jacksonville. Bobby scored four touchdowns in the first half in the game at the Orange Bowl and came off the field huffing and puffing after a 65-yard gallop. Farmer grabbed the panting youngster, shoved him into the shrubbery and said, "If you hadn't been smoking, you would have scored ten touchdowns!"

They talked of the crucial game with City in 1950. It was probably the most crucial in Farmer's career because City was making a comeback and Central had gone through two bad years after winning a state championship. They remembered the electrifying atmosphere in the city before the game, the tremendous crowd at Chamberlain Field and, of course, the surprisingly easy victory by the Pounders.

"How about Norman Hofferman," someone said. Norman was a great one and Farmer will never forget that Norman's mother wasn't interested in anything but grades. His sister was at City, but Norman wanted to go to Central and did. "Norman made his letter in the ninth grade," Farmer recalled and then he smiled. "He was proud of it and when he wore the letter home his mother remarked, 'see there, Norman, you can only make a C in football.'"

But, yesterdays are gone with only such memories remaining. It was party time and time to salute the last member of the Fearsome Foursome who would be saying his own goodbye to Central students for the last time two weeks hence.

Soloist Teresa Tate put the crowd into a fun mood with a rendition of "You Light Up My Life," just for Coach Farmer and ended it with a kiss. Brief salutes from special guests preceded a sudden commotion, resulting from a conspiracy between Bob Holmes, Buck Gaddis, Happy Mallett, Chink Brown and a dozen others that led to the "arrest and trial" of Farmer before the gathering with Ray Albright and Steve Bevil as opposing attorneys.

Gaddis and his jury rendered a verdict that led to the presenting to Farmer gifts that included a trip to Europe, a 20-year perpetual award in his honor with a plaque to the yearly winner, a football award in his honor and tickets to the Orange Bowl football game. There were proclamations, too, from state and local officials.

The speech Stan Farmer had planned to make was forgotten. The words would never have made it past his throat. It was the first time he had ever choked and that includes football, Iwo, Saipan and Tinian.

He had meant to say, "The main thing in my life has been the kids. Your steering committee has done a magnificent job. It has gone beyond all expectation showing appreciation for what I've tried to do.

"Listen, I'm not used to taking, I'd rather give and I'm really embarrassed to be on the receiving end.

"I can't say enough about Central people. Everything I've put into this school has been returned threefold. I accept this with deep humility.

"My wife and daughter will see that my hat will remain the same size."

What were Stan Farmer's secret thoughts? They must have been similar to those of Grantland Rice when he penned of himself:

"Where the old dreams move along,
Shadows that drift to and fro;
Moving on back through the years,
I've seen a pretty good show."

And a good show it was. It ran for 31 years for Stan Farmer and when it ended Saturday he got the standing ovation he deserves.

From the clan he loves so much.

For once the builder of boys into men became overcome with emotion and could not finish his prepared thank you speech. The famous "booming" voice became lost in the overflowing emotion that Coach Farmer was feeling. In reality no words had to be spoken as all in attendance knew the true love that he felt towards all of them, each in their own unique and special way.

When Coach Farmer died in September 1996, Roy Exum of the *Chattanooga News-Free Press* wrote a column eloquently covering the burial ceremony which included comments by former head coach and colleague E.B. "Red" Etter and several former players. All expressed their appreciation for the impact that Coach Farmer had on their lives. Some spoke about how he turned their lives around to make them productive citizens. Others recalled how Coach Farmer helped them to obtain a college education. All spoke from the heart as to the impact Coach Farmer had on their lives.

Even after death Coach Farmer stories continued to surface. Sportswriter Stephen Hargis stopped by Katherine Farmer's residence in East Brainerd to pick up a photo of one of the Central players to be included in the papers list of the greatest local football players. The short stop turned into an interview that produced additional information to add to the legend of Coach Farmer as to his unreported assistance to players and students at Central.

The late reporter Bill Casteel in 1997 wrote a story in his Byline column – "Coach A Legend in His Time" that added more incidents of the impact that Coach Farmer had on the lives of all he touched.

Wednesday, February 19, 1997

For questions or comments about this section, please call 752-3308.

Byline
Bill Casteel

Coach a legend in his time

Stanley Farmer must have been saint material.

I never had the good fortune of meeting the man, but I've heard and read nothing but good things about this late icon who for years patrolled the classrooms, principal's office and football field at Central High School.

It is always with reverence that those who knew him best speak of the man who became a legend in his time.

Many have been the times I have listened to attorney Jerry Summers express in adulatory terms his heartfelt feelings and respect for Mr. Farmer as an educator, a football coach and, most important, a friend.

For weeks preceding Mr. Farmer's death, radio sports talk show hosts, guests and callers lionized the legendary figure and his mate of many years, Katherine.

But it wasn't until I had a brief conversation with Alan Pressley, a defensive back for the Purple Pounders of 20 years ago, that I came to fully understand and appreciate how decidedly deep the love and admiration runs for the man whose "boys" still call him "coach."

The purpose of Alan's visit was to get out the word that his class of 1976 is joining other Central classes in the effort to raise money to endow a perpetual college scholarship in coach Farmer's memory.

He handed me a single sheet of paper that contained a summary of the goal he and a multitude of others like him hope to reach and how they plan to attain it.

Briefly stated, the aim is to raise between $50,000 and $100,000, with contributions coming essentially from those whose lives were touched by coach Farmer over the years.

The purpose of Alan's visit was to get out the word that his class of 1976 is joining other Central classes in the effort to raise money to endow a perpetual college scholarship in coach Farmer's memory.

He handed me a single sheet of paper that contained a summary of the goal he and a multitude of others like him hope to reach and how they plan to attain it.

Briefly stated, the aim is to raise between $50,000 and $100,000, with contributions coming essentially from those whose lives were touched by coach Farmer over the years.

I glanced at the paper and put it aside. It was then that Alan, perhaps thinking that I was less than impressed by his written words, started telling me how much coach Farmer had meant to him, how much he loved and continues to love the man who was such a positive influence in his life.

He tried to hide it, but there was a lump in his throat, perhaps a trace of a tear in his eyes.

I retrieved the paper — a copy of a letter he was sending out to his classmates — and read it more carefully.

"Each of us who had the privilege to know Coach Farmer loved him just as he loved us. The lessons that he taught the students and players at Central are reflected in the number of productive citizens in our community and beyond."

Right about then, I recalled an earlier meeting I had with Alan. It was in the winter of 1984, and he was performing for the kids at Orange Grove Center; doing his Elvis Presley — that's the one with only one "s" in his last name — impersonation.

It was a most appreciative audience and one that touched the heart of the performer. I remember tears trickling down his cheeks when, while mouthing the words to *My Way*, he made his way into the crowd and draped one of his scarves around the neck of a little wheelchair-bound child and kissed her.

I now suspect that Alan's compassion for those special children was somewhat a perpetuation of the exchange of love that existed between the "coach" and his "boys."

Folks wishing to help perpetuate the memory of coach Farmer's good deeds and help some deserving students get a college education should send their contributions to: The Central High School Alumni/Supporters, 5728 Highway 58, Harrison, Tenn. 37341.

Gifts are tax-deductible.

Bill Casteel's Byline column appears Monday, Wednesday and Friday.

Coach Farmer Recalls 31 Years of Loving Central

By STEVE PARKER
N-FP Staff Writer

The kids still call him "coach," though his days of instruction on football practice fields are long past.

Yet, it's the easy-mannered way he likes things run at his school, a school he has dedicated 31 years of his life to loving.

To those touched by the man, whether they received his guidance in battling opposing linemen on a football field or learned from him the value of motivation in daily endeavors, the knowledge that here is a special kind of educator remains a sweet memory of their high school experience.

And so do the bear hugs administered on "my kids" during his daily strolls down the Central High halls, where students in their own shows of emotion return the gesture of admiration and respect to "coach."

It's been a "marvelous love affair" between Principal "Coach" Stan Farmer and his charges and, though he will be retiring from Central and the field of education after this school term, "Coach" Farmer insists "I'll never really leave."

Indeed, his shared principles of "fairness," by which "everybody stands on their own two feet" and his display of "concern and interest" in each of 1,100 youngsters under his wing will remain as lasting monuments to "coach."

"For 31 years, I've never minded one time getting out of bed to come to Central," Mr. Farmer beams. "Sure with 1,100 kids it gets hairy sometimes, but I love them all and I'd do anything in the world for them. They have been my life."

Relaxing behind a cluttered desk of "Go Pounders" stickers, mementos presented him by admiring students and schedules of upcoming school events for the spring semester, "Coach" Farmer, in customary suit and tennis shoes, reviews his three decades at Central.

"Here, I've tried to create an atmosphere of fairness. If discipline had to be meted out, it would be done fairly. Everybody in this school stands on their own feet and when I had to become the disciplinarian, the students knew I played no favorites."

Football line coach under head coach E. B. "Red" Etter for some 23 years, Mr. Farmer became Central's assistant principal in 1971, serving in that capacity until being named CHS principal in 1976.

Only the fifth principal at Central since 1907, Mr. Farmer claims the transition from football coach to the school's top position "was not difficult," noting that, to young people, "coach" stands for warmth and leadership... there's a certain intimacy attached to 'coach' and I would never change that title with my kids."

While "Coach" Farmer admits school curriculum and discipline "are must haves," displays of interest in students on a personal basis are No. 1 in this man's book.

"They don't want a stiff type where his office is not enterable," Mr. Farmer smiles. "Here, they come to me at a moment's notice. I've learned through the years that as long as young people realize you care for them, why then discipline problems just vanish... just like that.

"Students know they can come by my office, talk to me and lay it all out on the table," he says. "There is nothing more important in the educational process."

Having such rapport with his students, Mr. Farmer points out that, through his experiences, "familiarity does not breed contempt.

"If I've ever had anything going for myself, it's that very few kids have taken advantage

Steve Parker column continued.

or lost respect for me, no matter how personally I knew them," Mr. Farmer says.

"I'm not a great intellect. never an honor roll student or cum laude, but I could always get along with people," he smiles. "I tried to show a man's love to those I cared for and it has always been returned to me twice fold."

A retired Navy commander, Mr. Farmer served as a Navy lieutenant on merchant ships in the North Atlantic theater, after becoming the first chief petty officer with no previous Navy experience ever to take a crew of 160 recruits through training.

The year was 1941, five years before his Navy discharge and return to Chattanooga.

"When I came to Central, I carried my desire to inculcate in kids the importance of their meaning something to parents, to Chattanooga, to the country, but mostly to themselves.

"I have always urged young people to make their presence known," Mr. Farmer says, "for the betterment of themselves and for everything they touch."

The normally soft-spoken, easy-going "Coach" Farmer admits "I can be explosive when I have to... and I have had to in the past," but he claims that normally a smile, clear of the throat and quiet "I want your attention" is enough "to gain the ear of most students."

But "Coach" Farmer says he is sensitive to discipline, noting that "if I've disciplined someone and I see that same person later on coming down the hall looking down at the ground and not caring to speak to me, I stop him.

"I'll tell him, 'Look, this is not something that continues. It was a corrective measure and now it's behind us, over with and, in my opinion, forgotten.' I try to explain to my kids, I'm trying to do what's best for you and, rest assured, I will never hold a grudge.'"

Mr. Farmer will end his Central career on July 1, leaving with young people the advice of 31 years' experience and "practical application.

"I want to tell my kids to have an objective in front of them and to always be true to themselves, to answer their own consciences," Mr. Farmer says. "And listen young people, treat the people you meet through life with fairness, always keep firmly in mind how they would want to be treated in the same instance.

"When confronting another, look at his or her background," he adds. "It will provide you with insights you hadn't realized before."

Mr. Farmer says perhaps his greatest awareness "acquired through teaching" is that students — the athletes, the intellectuals, the outspoken or the reclusive — "all want to be recognized, praised and appreciated.

"Sometimes the words you say fall on fertile ground and sometimes the seeds don't take," he explains. "But I have never known myself to be any different type of person through my successes or my failures. Being Stanley Farmer is all I know to be."

In his retirement, Mr. Farmer says he hopes to travel "and do the things my wife and I want to do.

"I know for sure I won't get up as early as I did these past 31 years," he laughs. "We'll just do the things that come naturally. But I'll miss Central, the faculty and mostly the kids I've come in contact with through all the years.

"So much of the understanding and love they received as they grew came right from Central High, and they put just as much right back in. There was mutual love, and I'll never forget the feeling."

Courtesy of Chattanooga News-Free Press

Coach Farmer In Hospital; Athletes Recall His Reign

By VAN HENDERSON
Free Press Staff Writer

Coach Stan Farmer's Purple Pounders used to take plenty of whippings, but seldom on the athletic field.

Throughout the 1960s and 1970s, Central High athletes got most of their school discipline from the "big bear of a man" who coached and taught them.

The recent hospitalization at Columbia-Parkridge Medical Center of the 83-year-old retired educator stirred such poignant memories of his influence on their lives that several of Coach Farmer's proteges shared them with us last week.

They so admirably recall the role of teachers in all our lives (and provide such a complement to the thoughts expressed by City Editor Emeritus Julius Parker in his column today on Page K2), that we want to share them with you.

"Coach Farmer has been one of the three most influential men in my life," said local Coca-Cola bottling company executive Don Rockholt.

"The other two are my dad (W.L. "Bud" Rockholt) and a Sunday school teacher (R.W. McKaig) I had when I was a kid."

For six years during his junior and senior high school years, Mr. Rockholt was a student or athlete of Coach Farmer. You might even say he was one of the coach's "whipping boys."

"I wasn't a bad kid, but I was into everything in the world," Mr. Rockholt recalled. "Somebody'd smart off to me and I'd hit 'em. I'd usually get my butt kicked. Then when they finished with me, Coach Farmer would lay into me with his paddle. I guess he's whipped me at least 50 times.

"But, you know, every time he whipped me, he'd wrap those big arms around me and say, 'Don, son, I love you, and if I didn't think you needed this, I wouldn't have done it.'"

A couple of Coach Farmer's former players ran into each other last week at Oscar's, a landmark restaurant not too far from the present Central High School on Highway 58.

"It was Ronnie Robbs, one of the best players that ever put on a Central football uniform," Mr. Rockholt said of his chance meeting with the fellow alumnus. "And the only topic of our whole conversation was Coach Farmer. That's how much 'Coach' means to us."

Central High Assistant Librarian Janet Pressley's son Alan was an eighth-grader at J.B. Brown Junior High when he met the legendary coach.

"I was standing in the hall staring at Central's trophy case when all of a sudden this big man walked up beside me there in front of the trophy case and said, 'Son, you're gonna play football for Central, aren't you?'" Mr. Pressley remembered.

The junior high linebacker became one of Coach Farmer's biggest admirer's, a co-captain of the Pounders, and wore Central's colors on the All-City team.

Coach Farmer then was also assistant principal to Principal Hobart Milleaps and was often heard over the school's intercom.

"I'd hear mine and some of my buddies' names called out over the PA (public address) system during home room for us to go to the office, and I knew we weren't being invited down to eat breakfast with the principal," Mr. Pressley said.

In fact, those summonses were usually for meetings with Coach Farmer's perforated-wood "board of education."

"After he paddled us, he talked to us and hugged us, said he knew we were good boys that just forgot how to act for a minute or two, and told us he was there for us if we ever needed him," recalled Mr. Pressley.

Despite his occasional application of sharp discipline, Coach Farmer is still warmly regarded by his former charges.

"We've always felt comfortable around Coach Farmer, whether it was over at his house for FCA (Fellowship of Christian Athletes) meetings 25 years ago or in his hospital room visiting with him and Mrs. (Katherine) Farmer," Mr. Pressley said. "I don't know of any of his former students and players that hasn't always known Stan Farmer is one of the best friends we've ever had."

Local attorney Jerry Summers met Coach Farmer as a high school sophomore after moving here from Florida, where he had been a three-letter athlete (football, basketball and baseball) and member of a state championship team.

"Coach Farmer was the first person to welcome me to Chattanooga," Mr. Summers said. "He was there waiting for us with a smile and a handshake shortly after we arrived here at 6 o'clock in the morning."

The kid and the coach became friends easily, as many people say Stan Farmer does with anybody.

Mr. Summers remembers that Coach Farmer demanded much only from those who seemed capable of achieving much. "He wanted people to be as good as they could be."

One such person was Paul "Bull" Chapman, an All-State tackle for Central.

"Coach got on 'Bull' one day and just stayed on him," said Mr. Summers. "When we hit the locker room at the end of practice, another player said, 'Bull, next time he rides you like that, why don't you just haul off and smack him?'

"You should have seen ol' Bull's expression," Mr. Summers recalled. "His face scrunched up, tears filled his eyes, and he said, 'I would if I didn't love 'im so much.'"

Mr. Summers said he wishes Coach Farmer could hear from everyone he ever taught or coached.

"To only note the respect and admiration a few of us have for him really fails to show just how big influence Coach Farmer has had on people as a coach, teacher, and friend.

"There are thousands of people who regard this man as one of the biggest influences in their entire lives," said Mr. Summers. "I'm sure my thoughts are the same as theirs when I say, 'Coach, we still need you. Get well.'"

A CENTRAL LEGEND: Retired Central High School coach and educator Stan Farmer is surrounded by several of his former athletes and students during a dinner honoring his 83rd birthday. Seated, from left, are: Rick Hansford, Toy Manis, Coach Farmer, Bob Brannon and Sterling Jetton. Standing, from left, are: Mark Lawrene, Mike Allen, Mack Crawley, Dr. Robin Smith, Paul Forgey, Alan Pressley and Dr. Hal Jones.

Courtesy of Chattanooga News-Free Press

All of those articles are included in their entirety in order that nothing will be omitted from the outpouring of the affection displayed toward Coach Farmer throughout his lifetime.

Chapter XIII

The End of an Era

After his retirement from Central as principal in 1978 Coach Farmer and Katherine travelled and continued to support Central. They always looked forward to being invited to any gathering of former players and students.

Over the years his health slowly deteriorated but running into any of "his boys" had a healing effect on his ailments.

A surprise birthday party, "C" Club reunions, or just a chance meeting at a restaurant or flea market always brought a smile to his face and the ever present inquiry as to how the former player-student and his family were doing. He swelled with silent pride when he was told of after graduation successes and consoled them if things were not going well. He often gave scholarly advice as to where help might be obtained to solve any temporary setback.

When his health problems continued to re-occur in September 1996, word of his condition spread amongst his legend of admirers and several went to his hospital room at Parkridge Medical Center on McCallie Avenue to pay their respects. Ironically the site where Parkridge sits was the former home of the Purple Pounders football playing surface, Frawley Field. It had served as the football stadium for those teams before it was razed and remained a practice field until

Central moved to a Glenwood facility in 1956. From Farmers first year at Central in 1947 until the stadium was demolished, the field resonated with Farmers booming voice urging the young linemen under his tutelage to try harder to develop their skills and abilities.

Just before he died, Coach started hallucinating on occasion. He claimed he had a guardian angel that nobody else could see that set on a table next to his bed. His daughter, Kathy, asked her father what was her name and he replied, "Esmeralda."

On his final journey to the hospital the family was sitting in the admission office waiting to be assigned a room and Kathy asked her dad if he had brought Esmeralda with him. He strongly said, "No I did not. She wasn't doing anything, and besides she was ugly as hell."

When the end finally came he was laid to rest on September 18, 1996, at the National Cemetery with the other military heroes who have served our country in defense of our freedoms. Speculation arose as to whether his longtime silence of not identifying his favorite or best players would be broken. Had he named a select group that would serve as pallbearers and carry him to his final resting place?

In typical Coach Stan Farmer fashion he left instructions that he wanted all of his former athletes-students to be honorary pallbearers and share in the honor as stated in an announcement in the *Chattanooga Times* on September 17.

When the final ceremony started, the walkway to the Navy-Marine Pavilion was lined with hundreds of former young men and women who had been privileged to have come in contact with Coach Farmer on either the gridiron or the class room. Each could silently hope and believe in their hearts that they were one of the unidentified favorites of the man who had impacted their lives.

Editorials and columns from both local newspapers reflecting Coach Farmer's life and the high esteem to which he was held by those who had the privilege to have come in contact with him are included in the appendix.

His longtime colleague and friend, Coach E.B. Etter, upon hearing of Farmers passing said, "He was a tough coach but all the kids liked him. He was probably the most-loved person in Chattanooga .... He had a nature about him that attracted people."

Roy Exum's column in the *Chattanooga News-Free Press* describing the reflections by Centrals former athletic greats (and not so greats) paints a big picture as to the respect and effect of Coach Farmer on the lives of so many former young people that he and his wife touched over the years.

Three former Central athletes who had become preachers were privileged to speak at the burial ceremony.

Royce Powell, '56, was a third baseman on two of the Pounders state championship baseball teams and was a forward on the basketball team was the main speaker. The ceremony closed with additional remarks by former football players.

The next speaker, end Buddy Norton, '59, had come to Central from Northside Junior High School along with George Shuford, Mike O'Brien, and Grady Wade. He attended Austin Peay University in Clarksville, Tennessee and later would ac-

CHATTANOOGA FREE PRESS   SPORTS   Thursday, September 19, 1996

Farmer Laid To Rest But Won't Be Forgotten

ROY EXUM

When word came on Monday that Stan Farmer had died, I kept scanning the obituaries, trying to find which ones of all those famous Central High football players would finally be chosen as his pallbearers.

Coach Farmer, as long as he was alive, would never tell his favorites, leaving instead a huge and mighty following of those who had once worn the familiar purple-and-gold jerseys to imagine that, yes, they most surely would have a place among those closest to the old man's heart.

But as Wednesday morning came, and the air at the National Cemetery held that September tingle usually reserved for Friday nights, bright gold carnations and held out, leaving word that all of his boys should help put him down.

So two long lines snaked from the funeral tent, all the way out to the road, and when the flag-draped casket was slowly drawn through their midst, men whose necks were once bigger than their waists cried like the "grass-cutters" once did during their first week of practice in the old "Dust Bowl."

Red Etter, perhaps the most brilliant football strategist ever in these parts, called his longtime assistant "the most loved man in Chattanooga," and a quick glance at the crowd showed that to be true.

You see, it was Etter who made Central High the most feared football team in the South, but it was Farmer, his ever-present motivator, who would inspire those on the line to knock an opponent's jaw up somewhere around their ear.

The coaching combination of Etter and Farmer was strong, but throw in Jake Seaton and Les Newton and it became downright heady.

"Coach Farmer coached at Central for 30 years and I don't think he ever learned a play," said one of

"Some men live and die and are never missed; some live and die and are never forgotten.

"As long as there is a Chattanooga, as long as there is a Central High School, and as long as there is a boy somewhere playing with a football, we will remember Coach Farmer."

— Pastor Bob Kelly

"(Stan Farmer was) the most loved man in Chattanooga."

— Red Etter

his greats, George Shuford, "but he knew boys like no one I've ever known.

"I bet that for over half these guys he was the most important person in their lives besides their daddies," said George, and perhaps that was an understatement, knowing the impact Coach Farmer had on both the boys and the girls at Central High School for so many years.

He was a big man, loud and gruff and tougher than pig-iron when you first met him. But as one day would lead to another, and those hot football practices would finally turn into one of those magical Friday nights, Stan Farmer became just about the best friend a young man could ever hope to have.

He had once carried a machine gun at Iwo Jima, going in with that first wave to hit the beach, and years later he'd tell his boys that he'd been scared, but that God had seen him through, and now all that mattered in life was this: "Head up! Tail Down! Feet Spread! Drive with your legs!"

That is how he taught Central High linemen, all right, but you'd be shocked at how many Purple Pounders have succeeded in life itself by ... well, driving onward and upward long after they'd left school.

Wednesday's funeral was glorious, with former players such as Royce Powell, Bob Kelly and Buddy Norton — pastors all -- at their very best before the hushed and emotional gathering. Nobody got there late, either, which is a further tribute to the lessons once learned at a place called Frawley Field.

"Coach Farmer was a patriot, a teacher in the finest sense, a wonderful family man, and he was devout, if in his own way," explained Jerry Summers, who has set up a scholarship fund in Coach Farmer's name.

"But I guess the thing that most people will remember about Coach Farmer is that he was a friend. There is no telling how many kids he'd take home to Katherine down through the years, kids

who would later amount to something, just because Coach Farmer cared when nobody else would," said the respected attorney.

The crowd at the funeral was like a who's-who of great athletes in Chattanooga. There were Ed "Raceborse" Nobles, the Phillips brothers and all the Robbs — Ronnie, Bill and Stan.

Judge Steve Bevil, who later played at Vandy, stood among the giants, and Ernie McCarson, always so full of fun, was testimony these men were not just mourning a coach, but an era as well.

Terry Parks and Chink Brown and Eddie Test — oh, they were all there — and Central's best were everything from fancy business suits with purple neckties to the blue jeans and work shirts that showed some had just slipped away from work to say goodbye.

Butch Harless, one of the toughest ever to grace a football field, allowed how he'd been kicked out of several schools before he ever got to Central, but that once Coach Farmer had thrown him through three or four lockers it dawned on him he'd met somebody tougher than he was.

"If it hadn't been for Coach Farmer," Harless has said since, "I'd have probably wound up in jail somewhere."

Then they told how Coach had one day called Shuford out of class, tenderly hugging George through a tough time when he thought he might quit football, and then later talked the University of Tennessee into taking a chance on him.

"I owe him so much," Shuford managed to say.

And, as the county commissioner spoke, it was the same thing everybody else in the crowd was thinking.

As pastor Kelly said, "Some men live and die and are never missed; some live and die and are never forgotten.

"As long as there is a Chattanooga, as long as there is a Central High School, and as long as there is a boy somewhere playing with a football, we will remember Coach Farmer."

Courtesy of Chattanooga News-Free Press.

cept the call to become a minster and pastored churches in the Atlanta, Georgia area.

Robert Kelly, '59, who came to Central from Eastside Junior High to play middle guard on defense and left guard on offense had received daily "personal" instruction from Coach Farmer. A rough and tough player at Central he found religion, attended Tennessee Temple University and had pastored large churches at Murfreesboro, Tennessee and Greenville, South Carolina, prior to his death.

Kelly closed with a summary of the thoughts that were concurred in by all in attendance, "Some men live and die and are never missed, some live and die and are never forgotten. As long as there is a Chattanooga, as long as there is a Central High School, and as long as there is a boy somewhere playing with a football, we will remember Coach Farmer."

Central Alumni Committee establishes Farmer Scholarship. Seated, Martha Faye Blabon, Kathy Farmer Ratz, and Katherine Farmer; standing, Warren Hill, Ron Chilldress, George Shuford, Robin Smith, Bob McCoy, and J. T. Vick. Photo Courtesy of Chattanooga Times FreePress.

In order that the memory of Coach Farmer would also be further perpetuated a committee headed by Central graduates and supporters during the administration of President Martha Faye Blabon of the Central High Alumni/Supporters Association created the Stan Farmer Scholarship at the Community Foundation of Greater Chattanooga. It is awarded to Central seniors every year to help further their college educations.

This tangible remembrance of Coach Farmer remains but the most important monument of his existence is in the hearts and minds of those he touched as young men and women and contributed to their growth into adulthood.

Photo courtesy of Jerry Summers.

A6 CHATTANOOGA FREE PRESS ★★★

Deaths & Funerals

Stanley Farmer Dies; Was Coach, Principal

Former Central High football coach and Principal Stanley Farmer — who challenged a generation of Central High athletes while also showing compassion for them — died today, Sept. 16, 1996, in a local hospital. He was 83.

Coach Farmer had been at Central High from 1947 until 1978 as a teacher, assistant coach, assistant principal and later principal.

Stan Farmer

During much of that time, he served as an assistant football coach to legendary coach E.B. "Red" Etter. Coach Etter was known as a cerebral coach with gentlemanly ways, while Coach Farmer was known more for "getting in the trenches" with the youngsters.

He would work them hard, his players said, but he also knew how to show them he cared. In a story in Sunday's *Free Press*, numerous players who had heard Mr. Farmer had been ill shared memories of his positive influence on their lives.

After hearing of his death this morning, longtime friend Coach Etter said, "He was a tough coach but all the kids liked him. He was probably the most-loved person in Chattanooga... He had a nature about him that attracted people."

At the time of his retirement as principal of Central High in 1978, some 300 people attended a special ceremony in his honor.

A graduate of Chattanooga High, he had attended and played sports at Emory and Henry College in Virginia.

Prior to coming to Central High, he had served as an assistant coach at City High and had also been in the business world.

He had been a high-ranking officer in the U.S. Navy during World War II and was later active in the Naval Reserve.

Memorial contributions may be made to the Stan Farmer Memorial Scholarship Fund, c/o Jerry Summers, 500 Lindsey St., Chattanooga, Tenn., 37401.

Arrangements will be announced by Chattanooga Funeral Home, East, where the family will receive friends Tuesday from 2 to 4 and 7 to 9 p.m.

Obituary courtesy of Chattanooga News-Free Press

Stanley Farmer

A graveside service for former Central High football coach and Principal Stanley Farmer will be Wednesday at 11:30 a.m. in Chattanooga National Cemetery with the Rev. Royce Powell, the Rev. Buddy Norton and the Rev. Bob Kelley officiating.

Mr. Farmer, who challenged a generation of Central High athletes, died Monday, Sept. 16, 1996, in a local hospital. He was 83.

Coach Farmer had been at Central High from 1947 until 1978 as a teacher, assistant coach, assistant principal and later principal.

During much of that time, he served as an assistant football coach to legendary coach E.B. "Red" Etter. Coach Etter was known as a cerebral coach with gentlemanly ways, while Coach Farmer was known more for "getting in the trenches" with the youngsters.

He would work them hard, his players said, but he also knew how to show them he cared. In a story in Sunday's *Free Press*, many players who had heard Mr. Farmer had been ill shared memories of his positive influence on their lives.

After hearing of his death, longtime friend Coach Etter said, "He was a tough coach but all the kids liked him. He was probably the most-loved person in Chattanooga... He had a nature about him that attracted people."

At the time of Mr. Farmer's retirement as principal of Central High in 1978, some 300 people attended a special ceremony in his honor.

A graduate of Chattanooga High, he had attended and played sports at Emory and Henry College in Virginia.

Prior to coming to Central High, he had served as an assistant coach at City High and had also been in the business world.

He had been a high-ranking officer in the U.S. Navy during World War II and was later active in the Naval Reserve.

He was preceded in death by his parents, Frank W. and Margaret Echols Farmer, and two brothers, Frank and Stewart Farmer.

Survivors include his wife, Katherine Farmer; daughter, Kathy Ratz, Chattanooga; and a sister, Betty Hitchcock, Flintstone, Ga.

Memorial contributions may be made to the Stan Farmer Memorial Scholarship Fund, c/o Jerry Summers, 500 Lindsey St., Chattanooga, Tenn. 37401.

The family will receive friends today from 2 to 4 and 7 to 9 p.m. at Chattanooga Funeral Home, East.

Announcement courtesy of Chattanooga News-Free Press

Chapter XIV

Conclusion

During a person's lifetime there are usually individuals who take the time to assist a person along the road of life. Whether we want to acknowledge it or not, they are there.

Such was Coach Stanley J. Farmer!

This effort to memorialize his life in this book is totally inadequate to document the effect that he had on the lives of so many. Some have been fortunate to realize how he helped us and had an opportunity to thank him before he died. Others did not have that chance but all would have to admit in their hearts that "Coach Farmer" was responsible for molding their lives in some way.

A quiet war hero, a tough and gruff football coach, concerned school administrator, and loving husband and father, he was really the caring father figure of thousands of young men (and women) who can proudly claim the title of "being one of his boys" (and girls)!

Stanly J. Farmer: We Called Him Coach

Warnock Pro
Type and Design by Karen Paul Stone

CPSIA information can be obtained
at www.ICGtesting.com
Printed in the USA
LVOW13s2108280717
542775LV00001B/1/P